The Threshold of Glory

Where Mortals Touch the Invisible

Contributing Authors

Sue Ahn

Bonnie Chavda

Pat Chen

Flo Ellers

Brenda Kilpatrick

Varle Rollins

Dotty Schmitt

Destiny Image® Publishers, Inc.
P.O. Box 310
Shippensburg, PA 17257-0310

"Speaking to the Purposes of God for This Generation
and for the Generations to Come"

ISBN 0-7684-2044-X

For Worldwide Distribution
Printed in the U.S.A.

This book and all other Destiny Image, Revival Press,
and Treasure House books are available
at Christian bookstores and distributors worldwide.

For a U.S. bookstore nearest you, call **1-800-722-6774**.
For more information on foreign distributors, call **717-532-3040**.
Or reach us on the Internet: **http://www.reapernet.com**

Endorsements

This book, *The Threshold of Glory: Where Mortals Touch the Invisible*, is an excellent compilation of the journeys of six special godly women in their pursuit for the Glory of God. The longing that God has placed in each one of them for His Presence has fueled their unique quest for *His Glory*.

—Dr. Fuchsia T. Pickett
Conference Speaker
Author of *The Next Move of God*

In a day when so many books are being written about God's Glory, it is refreshing to find one that is filled with Scripture from God's Word coupled with personal testimonies about experiencing the Glory. I am glad I didn't miss reading this one.

These seven anointed women of God bring to their readers clarity about the need for, the pursuit of, and the life changes brought about by experiencing His Glory. Each is unique in her own world and none attempt to form a pattern for the reader to follow. Yet in learning of their struggles and findings we are encouraged to persevere for the prize of the high calling of God promised to all that reach for it.

There is no age discrimination to dissatisfaction. Something has been missing in the lives of many of God's people as they hurry through day after day doing what is known as "business as usual."

We need to realize that we are standing on the threshold of the next move of God and that dissatisfaction is a necessary motivator for pursuit of that move. This book will point the way to finding that "secret place" for which we long. There, basking in His Presence, is where we are satisfied.

There is always a temptation to believe that we are different than anyone else. In this book you will read the testimonies of seven women very different from one another, yet with many similarities. Each desires more satisfaction and to find herself on the threshold of Glory. You will learn how to step over that threshold into His presence.

I highly recommend this book especially, but not exclusively, to women.

Iverna Tompkins
Author, Speaker

The Threshold of Glory is a book that beautifully confirms our joys in the Lord and our yearnings for more of the Presence of God. It clearly calls us to repentance, heart cleansing, humility, and holiness, and it encourages us to meet the daily trials and testings we encounter with gladness, to share the sufferings of Christ. This book builds in us high expectation for the greater glory that lies ahead.

Paula Sandford
Author, Teacher
Co-founder of Elijah House, Inc.

Contents

Preface

t is my privilege to introduce you to some very different, unique, and precious women of God. We all vary in age, education, experience, culture, and ethnic background. But we are deeply joined together in our singular passion and pursuit for the glory of His Presence. Indeed, we are each on a quest for His glory.

Each woman shares out of the richness of her own personal, spiritual journey and experiences of life. As you read these chapters, you will be both inspired and changed by the real-life testimonies of what happens when God actually shows up in a person's life. You will be thrilled by the accounts of how being saturated and soaked in the glory of His Presence produces a life-changing transformation. It is in the glory of His Presence that healing, deliverance, restoration, and empowerment take place.

Our God yearns to clothe us both within and without with His love, His gifts, His anointing, and, yes, with His very glory. The experience of His glory releases in us a fresh boldness to witness to His saving grace, and it imparts a deeper cleansing to live a pure life of holiness in all our relationships.

Each author, with great transparency and humble vulnerability, takes you into the broken places of her life. Fears, insecurities, and doubts are opened before you. It soon becomes so obvious that the glory of His Presence comes not to the perfect, but to the humble, to the broken, and to those who are thirsting for living water to come to the dry, parched places of their lives.

It is our united prayer that these pages will inspire you and impart to you a deeper hunger to be both a receiver and a carrier of His glory, and may your own exciting personal quest for His glory be a continuous journey of joyful discovery.

Dotty Schmitt

Foreword

This book could as well have been titled *The Quest for Glory*, but I'm glad it wasn't, because each woman testifies that though we are so thrillingly experiencing the wonderful Glory of God, we are only upon the threshold of what God is about to pour out. As I read, my heart and spirit leapt in hope—and in repentance for my own dryness. I suspect many will experience the same as they read, and for that I heartily recommend the book.

We have been reveling in joy as God has been raising the Church from its scattered dryness (see Ezek. 37). This book testifies that now we are about to move from waist-deep struggling into the refreshing, upholding waters that can only be swum (see Ezek. 47). Hallelujah for this time—and for this timely book.

This book is another in God's provision of inspiration and instruction for this time, in the genre of Tommy Tenney's *The God Chasers*, Dutch Sheet's *The River of God*, and Loren Sandford's *Prophetic Worship*. Our loving Lord is wooing us into His embrace, and giving us signposts like these along the way.

John Sandford
Author, Teacher
Co-Founder of Elijah House, Inc.

The author of two books, **The Delight of Being His Daughter** and **The Bride Wears Combat Boots**, Dotty Schmitt summarizes the two main passions of her life—learning to enjoy the healing of the Father's love and cultivating a deep intimacy of relationship with the Bridegroom of our soul—Jesus, the Son! Dotty continues to travel increasingly among God's people who are moving in revival power and anointing. She and her husband, Charles, senior pastor of Immanuel's Church, have been passionate expositors of the Scriptures for more than 40 years. Dotty has a degree in philosophy from Queens College in New York City, where she also attended Biblical Seminary. Her deep desire is to know the Lord more intimately and to experience the power of His Word in every circumstance of daily life. Dotty's love for the Word and for the glory of His Presence is imparted to all those to whom she ministers. She believes this is an awesome hour in which to love and serve the Lord. Dotty is also on the pastoral staff of Immanuel's Church and has a vision and burden for the Washington, DC area and the wider Body of Christ.

Chapter 1

The Longing Heart

Dotty Schmitt

Then Jesus said, "Did I not tell you that if you believed, you would see the glory of God?" (John 11:40)

Then Moses said, "Now show me Your glory" (Exodus 33:18).

For years the biblical concept of the glory of God has captured some of the deepest inquiries and longings of my heart. Early in my Christian experience I found myself pondering the inspiring events of Exodus 40 and Second Chronicles 5. In these awesome accounts the glory of God so filled the tabernacle and the temple that Moses and the priests, overcome by the "weightiness" of Jehovah's Presence, could neither enter nor stand in that majestic glorious Presence. The manifest demonstration of the glory of God always seems to result in at least three very distinctive happenings:

...and they worshiped and gave thanks to the Lord, saying, "He is good; His love endures forever" (2 Chronicles 7:3).

1

An unveiling of His glory to our hearts will always elicit from us deep worship, overflowing thanksgiving, and a clear prophetic agreement and proclamation that: "He is good; His love endures forever."

My own personal quest and pursuit after the "glory of His Presence" has been stirred greatly by the colorful life and inspiring example of the deep passion and spiritual pursuit of God's friend and beloved servant, Moses. The unfolding of this intense, intimate, and at times baffling and bewildering relationship between the Lord and his servant-friend Moses is most dramatically portrayed to us in Exodus 32 and 33.

Imagine for a moment dwelling and communing with the great "I AM" of the universe for 40 days and nights. During these intense days, Moses was receiving strategy and revelation from the God of glory. He was hearing the values, commandments, and heart of the Lord. He was receiving a detailed plan for the construction of a "dwelling place" for the Lord God Himself. How very amazing that even though the people only wanted to follow Him from a distance, the Lord Himself longed to "dwell among them" (see Ex. 25:8). What was Moses seeing, hearing, and feeling during those awesome and powerful days? How did he feel when he found himself clutching the two stone tablets inscribed by the very finger of God? One can only longingly and creatively imagine something of the intensity and glory of those intimate moments between Jehovah and His beloved friend and faithful servant.

Now move to the scene that took place among God's people at the foot of the mountain—events that were shocking, sobering, and very grievous. Tested by what they felt was too long a delay, the people became impatient and rebellious against Moses and against the Lord. (Repeatedly, the "delays" of God have been among the greatest tests for the people of God. How do we respond when He seems to take "too long"?)

Even Aaron was enticed into their rebellion and soon the idolatry and unfaithfulness of their hearts found expression in the forming of a golden calf. So grieved was the heart of the Lord that He pulled away in anger from His chosen ones. One of the most heart-wrenching interchanges occurred between Lord and servant. Neither one wanted to "own" these people! Jehovah referred to them as "your people" while Moses responded with, "They are Your people" (see Ex. 32). The very intense and deeply emotional scene between God and friend that followed this exchange must have been anguishing for both. See these events from the Lord's perspective. He longed to live and dwell among His people, but they were so sinfully self-absorbed that they could only live in the moment for their own pleasure. They were seemingly oblivious to the awesome plans and purposes that their God had prepared for them. The consequence of sin and disobedience is always ultimately judgment and death.

Yet in the midst of such a devastating scene, there was one very bright spot. The Lord's friend, Moses, arose as one who changed the very destiny of his nation through the power of his fervent prayers and daring intercessions. He boldly reminded the Lord that these were *His* people and that *His* name and *His* promises were at stake. The Scripture simply declares, "Then the Lord relented and did not bring on His people the disaster He had threatened" (Ex. 32:14).

In the midst of this very heartbreaking episode of sin, rebellion, and disobedience emerged one man who loved His Lord and His people and His purposes more than his own ambitions, yes, even more than his own life (see Ex. 32:31-32). What comfort and delight Moses must have brought to the grieving heart of his God.

Yet one last major obstacle remained before Moses. The Lord agreed not to destroy the nation, but their sin was so grievous that He could not yet bear to be among them. So the Lord proposed to send an angel before the people to lead them. But so essential was the very Presence of the Lord Himself to Moses that he could settle for nothing less, even if it were a blest angelic presence. We can observe in this that ascending journey of a soul in longing pursuit after more of his God—a man on a quest for God's glory.

I imagine that the traumatic events recorded in Exodus 32 and the first part of Exodus 33 left Moses feeling deeply lonely for an even more intimate revelation of this most awesome, as well as baffling, God that he had been called to love and to serve. For from his very depths came these two intense heart cries:

...Teach me Your ways....show me Your glory (Exodus 33:13,18).

It is obvious that all Moses' deep and emotional interactions with the Lord made him all the more aware of how much more there was to know of this great "I AM THAT I AM" (Ex. 3:14 KJV). So Moses, beloved friend and servant of the Lord, stood in His Presence with an intense yearning and longing. What was Moses asking for? And why was he so passionately seeking after the glory of the Lord?

I believe that it is in the Lord's answer to Moses that some clues are given to those of us who also have a quest for His glory burning deep within our souls (see Ex. 3:3-15; 33:19-23). The Lord speaks of His goodness, His very moral excellence. He proclaims His awesome name. He is the Lord, the great I AM of all the universe. But then He tells Moses to position himself in a most strategic place, "in a cleft of the rock" (Ex. 33:22 KJV).

I deeply suspect that when Moses was communing with Jehovah on that most holy mountain that he became increasingly suspicious that there was more to this awesome God than he was presently understanding or perceiving. I believe that at times he caught glimpses of a beauty, a majesty, a penetrating holiness that left him both speechless and seeking. In answer to Moses' cry and quest for the glory, the Lord placed him into the cleft of the rock. What did Moses see from within the cleft of the rock? Perhaps he received a deeper insight into the blood of the atonement and a greater revelation of the meaning of all the types and shadows to which he had been exposed on that Holy Mount. The writer of Hebrews also gives us some understanding of this most profound event when he writes of Moses, "...he persevered because he saw Him who is invisible" (Heb. 11:27).

Ever since mankind "fell short" of the glory of God in the Garden of Eden (see Rom. 3:23), all humanity has felt "uncovered." We not only lost our purity and innocence, but we primarily lost our

4

intimate access to the Lord of glory. His glory is so majestically holy that sinful man would be consumed in that glory, unless we once again receive a "covering." As Moses stood in the cleft of the Rock, I believe that he worshiped, as he more deeply understood the meaning of sacrifices, lambs, altars, and blood. Without the blood, there can be no glory! No wonder the noted hymnist August Toplady proclaimed this eternal truth even back in the midst of the eighteenth century:

> "Rock of Ages, cleft for me,
> Let me hide myself in Thee;
> Let the water and the blood,
> From Thy wounded side which flowed,
> Be of sin the double cure,
> Save from wrath and make me pure."[1]
>
> Augustus Toplady

Essential to the "quest for glory" is also the deep quest for purity and holiness. Moses was fervently longing for more of the manifest Presence of the Lord. He longed to know God more intimately. He cried out to see His glory. The Lord showed him His goodness, proclaimed His revelation name, and put him in the cleft of the rock. I believe that the beloved apostle John sums up his own quest for the glory when he so beautifully declares:

The Word became flesh and made His dwelling among us.
We have seen His glory, the glory of the One and Only, who
came from the Father, full of grace and truth (John 1:14).

So it has been throughout the ages; those of His people who have come to know Him through the awesome redemption of His blood, those who have come to experience His unconditional love through the baptism of His Holy Spirit, are left with an unquenchable longing and quest for more of His glory to be revealed. So it was for Moses and for John, and so it continues to be for all who follow in their pathways. The Lord will put us also "in the cleft of the rock." He will take us into a deeper revelation and appropriation of

---

1.   Robert K. Brown and Mark R. Norton, editors, *The One Year Book of Hymns* (Wheaton, Illinois: Tyndale House Publishers, Inc., 1995) p. July 19.

5

the cross of Jesus Christ. He will take us deeper into the profound atonement of the blood of Christ. As we receive deeper and deeper cleansing in His precious blood, and as we allow the cross of Christ to deal increasingly deeper with our self-life, He will unfold more of the awesome beauty of His manifest glory to us and in us.

Moses was not permitted to see the "face" of God (see Ex. 33:23). Amazingly, we who have received the good news of salvation and redemption through the blood of Jesus Christ are now able to see His face:

> *For God, who said, "Let light shine out of darkness," made His light shine in our hearts to give us the light of the knowledge of the glory of God in the face of Christ* (2 Corinthians 4:6).

Moses' "quest for glory" never ceased, even when in death he was "kissed" by God and taken into the eternal dimension.[2]

For me, personally, one of the saddest notes to be recorded in biblical history is the account of Moses becoming disinherited from entering the land of promise. What a travesty for Moses! His anger with the people caused him to become disobedient to the Lord. This time the verdict of the Lord was unrelenting: "...you will not bring this community into the land I give them" (see Num. 20:1-13; Deut. 3:21-29).

I can still vividly recall the very first time that these passages of Scripture washed over my heart and mind. I actually wept! How could this be? How could the Lord deprive His faithful servant of entering the land of promise? It certainly appeared that when Moses interceded on behalf of a whole nation, God heard and relented (see Ex. 32:14). Now pleas on his own behalf were emphatically denied: "...'That is enough,' the Lord said. 'Do not speak to Me anymore about this matter'" (Deut. 3:26).

---

2. The expression "...according to the word of the Lord" in Deuteronomy 34:5 (KJV) may also be translated "...according to the kiss of the Lord."

I can still remember sitting, feeling rather perplexed and bewildered before the Lord concerning Moses' judgment. I asked, "Lord, how could You allow this to happen to him? It just doesn't seem fair!" Even after I had read all the different theological explanations and biblical commentaries on the subject, my heart was still largely dissatisfied. No wonder Moses had cried, "Teach me Your ways"— for the ways of God appeared to become even more baffling and bewildering the more determined one became in this holy quest for the very glory of His Presence! The Lord's response to my impassioned inquiries concerning His dealings with His beloved friend was complete silence—at least until many months later when I was no longer inquiring intensely concerning this matter. However, the Lord finally chose to speak the revelation of His word on this matter deep into my heart.

I was in a simple prayer gathering with a few of the older saints of God. In the midst of our prayers, a sister arose to her feet and began reading the transfiguration account from Matthew 17. Jesus was up on a high mountain in the very land of promise when Moses and Elijah appeared, talking with Jesus about "His departure." (Luke also beautifully records this event and writes concerning the three disciples: "...they saw His glory and the two men standing with Him..." [see Lk. 9:28-36].)

As the sister read these words, the revelation voice of the Lord penetrated deep into my soul. "Yes, My daughter, Moses did stand in the land. He stood in the very Presence of the One he had always longed after and he saw His glory." With that living word to my heart, I simply fell on my face and wept and worshiped. Such love filled my heart for this majestic, loving God. No wonder Paul wrote:

Oh, the depth of the riches of the wisdom and knowledge of God! How unsearchable His judgments, and His paths beyond tracing out! (Romans 11:33)

I learned something very precious about our tender, loving God. He desires not only to answer the honest inquiries of our minds, but He always longs to answer the yearnings of our hearts to more intimately know Him and the beauty of His ways.

On that simple, ordinary day, many years ago, in the midst of a humble home prayer meeting, I was changed from deep within. The Lord Himself met some of the deep cries of my heart to know Him and to love Him more intimately. He changed me by taking me deeper into the knowledge of His ways, and He lifted me higher into the glory of His very Presence. Isn't it interesting to observe that every precious encounter of our souls with our beloved Lord only serves to increase our thirst and quest for more of the glory of His Person, of His Power, and of His very Presence. Nothing else will ever satisfy! No one else will ever satisfy! Along with the disciples of ages past, we, too, continue to cry: "We want to see Jesus!"

We are presently living in "seasons of refreshing." There is a fresh river of life flowing freely from the throne of grace for all who are thirsting for more. All over the earth God's people are worshiping with this very powerful refrain: "Oh the glory of Your Presence...." It certainly seems as if the Lord is drawing near and once again kissing the earth with the glory of His Presence.

For me, this fresh kiss of His Presence upon my life occurred early in March 1994. For months, a handful of intercessors had been meeting regularly on Monday mornings. The longer we prayed together, the more focused and intense our intercessions became for more of His refreshing, revival Presence to become manifest among us, especially among our children. For years the account of the 1950's revival in the Hebrides Islands had deeply stirred and inspired my heart to believe God to "do it again" here and now. The rhema promise given to the two elderly Smith sisters at that time was from Isaiah. Our small intercessors group also began to claim this powerful promise for revival:

> For I will pour water on the thirsty land, and streams on
> the dry ground; I will pour out My Spirit on your offspring,
> and My blessing on your descendants (Isaiah 44:3).

In March 1994, the winds of revival began to blow through our congregation. God began with our children and then fell upon the adults. One of the prophetic words given to this small group of intercessors was: "I will ignite the kindling first, and then the logs will catch the fire."

Even though I had been at the forefront of praying and interceding for revival and for more of His manifest Presence, when He did suddenly come on that weekend in March, I found that I was somewhat bewildered, confused, and skeptical about some of the manifestations that seemed to accompany His coming. Laughter, weeping, shaking, trembling, and people falling all over the place was not what I was asking for. By temperament I love deep, quiet times of worship. I treasure the old hymns of the church. I love to be in silence in the awesomeness of His Presence. However, He seems to enjoy seeing our formulas for proper church protocol shaken up a bit—just read the many accounts of authentic moves of revival. (All these manifestations, I have learned, also continue to be part of His kissing the earth.)

By the first Sunday evening, I had become rather exhausted by all of my analyzing and attempts at discerning what was happening. On one hand, I was thrilled by what was sovereignly happening among the children. Yet, at times it all seemed rather confusing as well. After all, wasn't our God a God of order and not of confusion (see 1 Cor. 14:33)?

On that eventful Sunday evening, I stood at the altar for prayer along with the rest of our pastoral staff. Soon, I realized that I was among the few who remained standing. That was fine with me, except that I knew that I needed something more from the Lord. He seemed to be passing me by! I remember crying out, "Lord, it's You that I want. I don't want experiences. I don't even want the blessings of Your hand. Oh, Lord, please, I hunger for more of You." It was as if my heart were crying out to Him, "Lord, remember my quest for Your glory."

Once again, the gentle voice of my Good Shepherd spoke deeply into my thirsty spirit. "My daughter, stop analyzing it all. I want a deeper yieldedness from you, and I want you to learn how to receive from Me at a deeper level of your being." With those words piercing my spirit, I forgot about everything and everyone else. It was the Lord and I interacting on a deeper level of yieldedness and receiving. I can still remember lifting my hands up as a sign of a fresh surrender to His total lordship. I then opened my hands in a receiving position and whispered, "I receive from You a fresh baptism of Your love. Enlarge the capacities of my heart to receive more of Your love, mercy, and grace." With that interchange between the Lord and myself, Paul's words took on new meaning:

And hope does not disappoint us, because God has poured out His love into our hearts by the Holy Spirit, whom He has given us (Romans 5:5).

As I stood there learning anew how to yield and how to receive, the Lord lavishly poured out His love into my heart. Even though the details and experience of these encounters often differ from one individual to another, the Lord knew that in my case, He needed not only to fill my hungering heart but also to still my skeptical mind! At that very moment of fresh yieldedness and deeper receiving I was thrown backwards to the floor, shaking and trembling as I had never done before. In fact, it was as if I had been hit by a spiritual tornado! I don't know how long I lay there, but I do know that I was basking afresh in the glory of His Presence.

After some time, when I did finally get up from the floor, I was changed, permanently changed! I loved Him more, I became more sensitive to what grieved Him, and a whole new dimension of the fear of the Lord, which is to hate evil, gripped my soul (see Prov. 8:13). In addition to this, there was released in my life a new boldness and confidence to witness and a greater anointing to minister life and healing to His people. No wonder Peter could say to the crippled man: "Silver or gold I do not have, but *what I have* I give you..." (Acts 3:6). I understood so much more clearly that night that the Lord yearns to pour His love mightily into our lives so that He can, in turn, pour out through us into the lives of a lost and hurting world.

Through the course of passing time, I have also continued to learn more deeply the truth that "the just shall live by faith" (Rom. 1:17 KJV). Our daily Christian life, with all its challenges, trials, and tests, gives us constant opportunities to make choices that will either sustain and cultivate the anointing and glory of His Presence or diminish and grieve His glorious Presence. Presently, I sense that He is teaching us how to welcome the glory of His Presence into the midst of our everyday lives.

Thank the Lord for all those dynamic revival encounters with the Lord, but thank Him even more for those daily opportunities to carry the fragrance of those precious encounters into our homes, our work places, and our neighborhoods.

From the challenging and inspiring account of Moses' quest for glory, we learn many life-changing truths. From each individual's personal search and yearning for more of an intimate union and communion with this Lord of glory, we learn some profound truths:

Seek the Lord while He may be found; call on Him while He is near (Isaiah 55:6).

We are living in a sovereign season of time when He can be found, a time when He is near. As we respond to His yearning to pour out more of His love upon us, we will continue to be powerfully and lastingly changed:

But we all, with open face beholding as in a glass the glory of the Lord, are changed into the same image from glory to glory, even as by the Spirit of the Lord (2 Corinthians 3:18 KJV).

So the quest for glory will ever continue! For it is a quest for an ever-deepening revelation of the Lord of Glory Himself! So throughout our lives, as well as throughout all of eternity, there shall continue to arise out of the hearts of the redeemed the wonderful and joyful cry of worship and adoration:

"Teach us more of Your ways....show us more of Your glory."

"Lord, thank You for the glory of Your awesome ways. Thank You for capturing our hearts with the glory of Your unconditional love, grace, and mercy. Thank You that Your grace is always amazing."

Brenda Kilpatrick and her husband have been Senior Pastors at Brownsville Assembly of God since 1981. She was called to be a pastor's wife at age 18 through a dream the Lord had given her mother. The Lord had shown her mother that if Brenda would completely give her life to Christ, she would be happier than she could ever imagine. But if she chose to rebel and go her own way, she would have a life filled with hardship and pain. Soon after that, Brenda gave her heart completely to the Lord. She met a handsome young man named John Alton Kilpatrick, who God had called to be a pastor. They fell in love and were happily married. They have been married 29 years and have been blessed with two sons, Scott and John Michael, two daughters-in-law, Karen and Elizabeth, two grandsons, Zachery and Austin, and a granddaughter, Bethany. Preceding the outpouring of the Holy Spirit at Brownsville Assembly of God on Father's Day, 1995, Brenda received a mighty touch from God that changed her life. She is a strong prayer warrior, and the Lord has anointed her to go out and minister to others as He opens doors.

Chapter 2

House Calls

Brenda Kilpatrick

ow many of you would like God to visit your home? Every one of you, I am sure! In the Old Testament we read of "house calls" that were made by God to two separate families. The first was to Adam and Eve. In Genesis 3 we read how God came to the Garden of Eden in the cool of the evening to walk and talk with them. Later, we read how the devil also visited the garden, entreating Eve to pledge her loyalty to him rather than God. Then God made his last "house call" to them. In Genesis 3:8-11, we read:

> *Then the man and his wife heard the sound of the Lord God as He was walking in the garden in the cool of the day, and they hid from the Lord God among the trees of the garden. But the Lord God called to the man, "Where are you?" He answered, "I heard You in the garden, and I was afraid because I was naked; so I hid." And He said, "Who told you that you were naked? Have you eaten from the tree that I commanded you not to eat from?"*

Isn't it interesting to note that no one had to tell them that they were naked! They could feel that the *chabod*, the weightiness, the glory of God, had been lifted from them. After this, they were evicted from the garden, the only home they had ever known.

Another "house call" that God made was to Obededom. In Second Samuel, chapter 6 we read of King David's desire to bring up the Ark of the Covenant out of the enemy's camp and back into the midst of His people. However, David did not approach the Ark God's way, but he used man's method to fulfill a godly desire, and in the process Uzzah was slain. David found himself bewildered and fearful by the Lord's doings and decided to have the Ark sent to Obededom's house. For three months, the household of Obededom enjoyed the Presence of God; everything they put their hands to prospered.

David's desire to find a resting-place for the Ark of the Covenant did not diminish. He sought God's way of approaching the Ark and brought it back to Jerusalem. However, through his own experience, Obededom had become accustomed to the Presence of the Lord and was willing to do anything to remain near it, even to the point of volunteering to be a porter, a singer, and even a doorkeeper.

Before Brownsville's sweet visitation of the Presence of the Lord, there were prophecies, dating back as far as 1989, that described God's desire to do a great work in our church. However, before a visitation from the Lord would come, we had to prepare for it, make straight paths before us, and "clean our houses."

What about your house? If Jesus came to visit you, would He feel welcome? Is there anything hindering the Presence of the Lord from being wherever you are? We need God's glory in our homes as well as in our churches.

My Visitation

For five months I took care of my mother-in-law, lovingly referred to by our children as "Big Mama," who was terminally ill with cancer. She was living in a nursing home, and I would go there each day just to comfort and be of help to her. It was my way of saying "thank you" for all the help she had been to me over the years. John and I are deeply devoted to our family and feel that we should be there for them when they need us.

During this period of time in our lives, my husband heard that there was a move of God in Toronto. He encouraged me to go check it out, promising that he would take over the care of Mom while I was gone. I agreed to go, and my friend Shirl and I flew to Toronto for a few days to see what God was doing there. I did not know what to expect, but I had heard that God was in the house and I wanted more of Him.

Even though their worship was different from what I was used to, I enjoyed the Pentecostal style. The music was great. Banners were waving. People danced before the Lord and teenagers jumped. I knew that this was God! During my first evening service there, I became very sleepy and felt that I must be weary from the traveling. Later, I learned that what I thought was tiredness was in actuality the *chabod* of the Lord, the weightiness of His Presence.

My friend and I wanted to be fresh to receive from the Lord the next day, so we did not stay until the end of the service for prayer. We returned the next evening, and again, we enjoyed the music and worship time. But I was desperate and said to the Lord, "If You are in this place, You had better come to me in the prayer line because I do not feel a thing!" We went and stood on the marked line and waited for God. A young lady came up to me and asked, "What do you need from the Lord?" I said, "I am a pastor's wife, and I am here for a refreshing."

She started to pray, but she never touched me. Immediately, I felt an intense heat on the top of my head that stopped at my neck. My toes went up, and I braced myself because I was not into "courtesy falls." I knew that if I ended up lying on the floor that I wanted it to be the result of a touch of God, and amazingly, I found myself on the floor! My friend told me that I laid on the floor for 45 minutes.

That was a miracle in itself, as I had previously had back trouble, but not after that night—the Lord completely healed me!

When I tried to get up off the floor, I could not, for I was "drunk" in the Spirit. This was a whole new experience for me. As I sat there, I felt so silly! As I looked around me there was a woman to my right, slightly overweight, whose abdomen was quivering like Jell-O. She vacillated between groaning and jerking. This happened over and over again, and in my spirit I knew God was healing deep wounds in her. As I looked to my left, there was a young woman in her twenties screaming, " No, No!" I sensed that she had been violated as a child and for the first time she was being set free. I heard laughter all around me. I also saw a man whose hands were trembling and shaking with such force that it amazed me. Nothing I saw or experienced that night offended me, and I knew that in just one hour God was doing what no doctor or psychiatrist could ever do.

My friend helped me up off the floor and back to our hotel room. We flew home the next day, not really knowing what God had done for me or what the future had in store.

The next Sunday morning, my husband wanted Shirl and I to share about our trip to Toronto with our congregation. Shirl and I had agreed beforehand not to mention anything about the physical manifestations we had observed. We wanted a sovereign move of God to come in whatever fashion He chose without influencing the people by relating the specific manifestations we had seen. We shared with them how 3,000 people had come to Toronto from all over the world with great expectation for healing and deliverance and that they had not been disappointed! My husband encouraged the people to praise and thank the Lord for the soon-coming revival. (After all, the Brownsville congregation had been seeking God for two and one-half years at this point, praying for revival around prayer banners.) Then my husband asked everyone to be seated, and he began his message.

One woman in our congregation named Georgia, who had been a barmaid prior to her salvation just one year earlier, remained standing, while my husband preached. She remained standing for 45 minutes with her eyes closed and her hands shaking, just like the man in Toronto! I was so excited that I wrote Holy Spirit a note that said, "Oh, Holy Spirit, You are here just like You are in Toronto. Make our congregation as hungry for You as Georgia is. Oh, please send revival to us!" Later, I found out that near where Georgia was standing in the sanctuary, Hazel, a member of the praise team, had fallen to the floor under the power of the Holy Spirit. Then a man, who had observed a horrible event at the age of eight and had been unable to cry since that time, began to weep.

One week later, I realized that I had received more than just the experience of being drunk in the Spirit; I had been set free! I had had strongholds in my life that I was dealing with, such as past hurts, a false image of myself, feelings of unworthiness, guilt, and shame. I even felt that my husband could have accomplished more in the ministry if he had chosen another wife. I believed the lies of the devil! You see, when I was 18 and away from God, my mother had a dream from the Lord. He told her to tell me that if I would come to the Lord, I would eventually marry a minister who had great wisdom and that I would be happier than I had ever been. Somehow, I forgot about the promise of marrying a preacher and being happy, but I did give my heart to the Lord and I started going to church. Then our family moved to Columbus, Georgia, where my father was in the army. I began attending Riverview Assembly of God, where I eventually met and fell in love with a handsome young man who for 31 years now has been a gift from the Lord to me.

We married and went away to Bible college for two years, and I became pregnant while in college. Our funds were low, and I realized that a diet of eggs, oranges, and grapefruit was not the type of nourishment that a baby inside me would need. So we left college and went back to Georgia. When our son Scott was nine months old, we took our first church in Vidalia, Georgia. I was brand new in ministry and did not really know what was expected of me. Worse yet, I had no mentor. I wanted to please everyone and be a good pastor's wife. I tried so hard to fulfill all the demands of the ministry.

I look back to those days and realize that I was a shy young girl who became intimidated early on in our ministry, and it really hindered my spiritual progress. One thing I had, though, was a lot of love for people. I had never liked cliques and always tried to make people feel special.

We have pastored four churches in 28 years of ministry and have experienced many things. Because of hurt in my life, I built walls to protect my heart. There was so much jealousy in the ministry. I missed having a pastor's wife to fellowship with, and I felt very alone. I was hurting and had no one to talk to. Fitting into all the "different hats" that women in ministry are expected to wear was very stressful to me. Over the years, I would cry to the Lord, "Why do I feel this way?" I felt as though I had done something wrong and had offended God. I listened but the Lord was silent. I never stopped reading the Bible, and I would repent, confess, and stand on the Word the best I knew how to do. I became discouraged and gave up on myself, but I never gave up on the hope I had in the Lord. Romans 5:5 (KJV) says, "...hope maketh not ashamed," and Isaiah 49:23 (KJV), "...*they shall not be ashamed that wait for Me.*" I tried to do what was right, but I failed to measure up to my own expectations. My righteousness was as filthy rags. I was like a car in need of an oil change. God wanted to purify me and give me fresh oil.

These are the reasons that I can say whenever I am out speaking at an engagement that revival didn't come to Brownsville because of John and Brenda Kilpatrick or Steve and Jeri Hill. By the time revival came, we were glad to give all the glory to the Lord. All John and I can take credit for is having our two wonderful sons.

In First Timothy 1:12 (KJV), we read, "And I thank Christ Jesus our Lord, who hath enabled me, for that He counted me faithful, putting me into the ministry." I can testify that *He* has enabled me to do what He has called me to do. After coming back from Toronto, I began to have an intimacy with the Lord that I never knew was possible. I love John Kilpatrick, but this intimacy with the Lord was different. This relationship was so deep and satisfying in my spirit. The Lord would awaken me as in previous times, but now it was different.

There was an excitement and anticipation to meeting with **Him**. On many occasions, I would wake up in the morning, go to my den, and kneel down in front of my recliner. I would lay my head down as if it were in my Father's lap. Then I would say, "Father, here I am." Immediately, His Presence would come over me. The warmth of His love would surround me. It felt as if I was a teabag in a teapot enveloped by the warm water of God's Presence, becoming saturated in His glory. Sometimes I would spend up to four hours before the Lord. I had prayed for years that the Lord would touch me and change my heart. I wanted to be pure and to please Him, and then when the Lord did touch me, no words could be spoken. There were only tears of gratitude and feelings of deep love for Him. I felt waves of glory come over me. It was so intense that at times I recall saying to the Lord, "If You don't stop, I'll die right here!"

Housework became less of a priority as I spent more and more time in the Lord's Presence. One day I was in the laundry room putting clothes in the washer and I remember asking the Lord, "Did You know how much I loved You and served You when I did not feel You? And now do You know how much more I love You since I can I feel You all the time?" You see, praying became easy, and immediately upon kneeling, I felt His Presence. The Bible became alive to me. I experienced a new level of worship, and I began to enjoy the freedom of dancing before the Lord in our home. My husband would come home and see me dancing. My new level of intimacy with God began to increase his hunger for the Lord. I had four wonderful months of intimacy at this level with the Lord before revival broke out at Brownsville. (Oh, how I pray that each of you will experience the Presence and intimacy of the Lord in this manner!)

We continued to pray for revival on Sunday evenings, and the women had an additional prayer meeting on Thursday mornings, finding their own special spot in the sanctuary to seek the Lord.

One Thursday, I left the sanctuary to go to the bathroom, where I saw two friends with whom I wanted to share a Scripture that the Lord had given me from His Word. I asked them to come into the pastor's lounge, and as I began to read the Scripture, I felt

21

waves of glory come on my head. I bowed my head and said, "Oh, I feel the Lord!" I was frozen in that position for the next two hours. I could not speak, although I heard the ladies ask each other what had happened to me. Shirl, who had accompanied me to Toronto, tried to explain how God had touched me. A little later, my husband came in and asked, "What is wrong with my wife?" The ladies explained that I was talking about the Lord and that now I had been in this position for hours. With this explanation, they excused themselves to pick up their children from school.

My husband sat down on the couch and asked a profound question, "Are you all right, and do you think you can come out of this? We need to leave now because I have a board meeting tonight." I *really* tried to open my eyes, so much so that my eye sockets were sore for days. He began to rub my back. I suppose he was hoping that it would increase my blood circulation. Then he began to laugh and say, "Well, this must be the Lord!" All of a sudden, I began to laugh, and I saw a vision of a donkey with its mouth wide open laughing and guess what…that donkey was me! This laughter was new to me, and it sure wasn't very ladylike! It was gut-wrenching laughter that came between weeping and crying and then laughing again. John finally managed to help me to the car and get me home. We changed clothes and went out to eat at a local cafeteria.

While eating our meal, my husband looked at me and said, "You know, Brenda, if this happened to anyone else, I wouldn't believe it. But because I know you and I know your life, I know God is going to send revival to our church!" And with that statement, before God and everybody in the restaurant, my husband began to weep! I laughed, knowing that he would never do anything in public like this outside of a divine touch of God. It was wonderful to see God touching him! Not only was my husband hungry for God, but the Brownsville staff members also began to hunger for more of the Lord. Most of them planned their own trip to Toronto and were mightily touched by the Lord.

On Father's Day, June 18, 1995, we at Brownsville experienced a visitation from our heavenly Father. Our church was forever changed, and now, over four years later, over three and one half million people have come from all over the world for more of the Lord. Over 134,000 people have been saved. Many people in a backslidden condition have come home, others have been healed and delivered, and this continues in every service to this date.

From the first day of revival, my husband declared, "Folks, this is it! Get in, this is what we have been praying for!" And with this declaration, and with no one touching him, he fell to the platform in the Spirit, where he remained for four hours! He said later that it was like when your grandma would put those heavy quilts over you at night when you slept at her house. That is exactly what the Lord did for him that day; He kissed John and said, "Now rest!"

It was around 4:00 in the afternoon when John got up off the floor and our youngest son, John Michael, helped him to the car. He sent John Michael back for me because we would be returning for the 6:00 service. I told our son, "Tell your dad that I don't mean to be disrespectful, but we've prayed for two and one-half years for God to show up and I am not about to leave just in case He doesn't come back tonight!"

Revival is awesome! Being able to witness souls coming to the Lord and their lives so miraculously changed and transformed is wonderful! The testimonies that are expressed when these precious people get into the baptismal pool are incredible!

Now I truly know what "church" should be like. This is harvest time, the greatest time the earth has ever seen, and the Brownsville Outpouring is only a small portion of what God is going to do in the earth. I believe that it is only a prototype of what God wants to release into all the churches today! The glory of the Lord was so strong in the early days of the revival that my husband and I both would find ourselves weighted with the *chabod* of the Lord the whole service: I would fall over or sit for hours without moving or opening my eyes, even though I could hear everything! My husband would lay his head over on a chair because he could not hold his head up. John Michael invited a friend to the revival and then asked

23

his friend how he liked the meeting. The friend replied, "I think it's cool, but why did your dad sleep all the way through the service?"

A Changed Family

Revival has changed our family! My husband, John, moves in a greater anointing as he speaks to pastors throughout the country. The boldness that I have to speak in front of groups is very significant for me. Before I experienced revival in my own life, I would have never felt comfortable on a platform.

Scott, our oldest son, has been changed! He had been hurt by unkind remarks made by members of a previous church we had pastored. As a family, we made it a point never to talk about people or about church problems. Pastor's children hear enough, believe me! He became suspicious of people.

Scott works at the United Parcel Service. After revival began, Scott, after working hard all day, would come to church to help us by playing the drums. One night, I looked at him playing the drums, and he looked so tired. I asked the Lord, "Are You going to touch everyone else's kid in this revival but not touch Scott?" Two weeks later, a friend asked him to go to prayer meeting. He attended and received the baptism of the Holy Spirit. He was so excited, and that was the beginning of a fresh touch of the Lord's glory in his life! Scott decided to go to the next prayer meeting, and there he asked the Lord to give him a vision like others had experienced. The Lord said, "Visions be loosed."

Scott saw Jesus standing in a wheat field calling his name, saying, "Scott, come here!" Scott ran to Jesus. They embraced and then began to run and roll in the wheat field together. I believe that Jesus was playing with our son as a way of healing all those old wounds. Then Scott saw a rainbow that came into the wheat field, and he asked Jesus, "Where does the rainbow go?" The Lord answered, "Heaven. Heaven is near." Again, Scott returned to the prayer meeting. He went to the back of the balcony to lay face down before the Lord. He asked the Lord, "Would You give me another vision?" Again, the Lord's reply was, "Visions be loosed."

Once again, he was in the wheat field, but this time, the scenery was different. There were snowcapped mountains surrounding the wheat field. Scott asked the Lord, "What are those mountains?" The Lord replied, "Those are My prayer warriors." Scott asked, "Lord, does the snow on top of the mountains mean that our prayers are cold and frigid?" The Lord answered, "Oh no, I'm the *Son* that melts the snow that nourishes the harvest!"

As the Lord spoke to him that day, Scott could see the snow melting and running down the sides of the mountains. The Lord continued, "And without the prayers and supplication of My people, the harvest would be lost." That is why the Lord has sent renewal and revival to the land. He had to touch us first and get us back on track so that we could finish the work needed to bring in the harvest. (See Psalm 126:1-6.)

(Scott has a beautiful wife Karen, who was also filled with the Holy Spirit during this revival. They have given us the privilege of being grandparents to two grandsons, Zachary and Austin, and then during this revival, we have been blessed with a "revival" granddaughter named Bethany, whose name means "House of Prayer.")

Our youngest son, John Michael, has been touched by the Lord and has been seen shaking under the power of God. He married Elizabeth Ward, who has shared her testimony on video. She told what a "snot" she had been until she had a tremendous three-day encounter with the Lord. They both work for our ministry, "Partners in Revival," and they often minister in other areas of the country together.

Elizabeth is a tenderhearted young woman who loves all creatures above and below the earth. She will take a jar and let a spider crawl into it and then release it outside so it can go free. Not me! I have no mercy toward creeping things that get into our home. In fact, one morning as I was going to my car, I saw a grasshopper on the car door. Before I thought about it, I flicked it off, stepped on it, and heard it "crunch." I immediately thought of Elizabeth. I said,

"Oh, Lord, I'm just killing everything!" The Lord spoke to me, "That's because you don't know the purpose of it."

How many of us truly know our purpose in life? God created us to live in fellowship with Him and to experience His glory. Likewise, God had a plan and purpose for the Tabernacle after Moses completed every requirement, but it all would have been useless without the glory of His Presence inhabiting the Tabernacle.

Obededom experienced the glory of the Presence of the Lord, and his purpose in life was changed forever. He made every necessary change to remain in God's Presence and to do His will, even to the extent of changing occupations and where he and his family lived.

Our family, too, will never be the same, after experiencing the Lord's glory. These four years have changed the purpose and destiny of our family forever!

Revival glory is wonderful, but God's intention and purpose is so far greater than manifestations or Christian festivals. It is for *SOULS*! God's purpose for His Church is to offer the glory of God to the lost and dying world. Without that vision, our church efforts are useless.

My prayer is "Lord of the Harvest, send Your glory down and raise up laborers for Your work."

Pat Chen is an ordained minister of the gospel at Harvest Church and is recognized as an apostle of prayer. She is founder and president of First Love Ministries International Inc. In ministry for over 20 years, Pat travels nationally and internationally. Her passion is for the Lord and His people, and her message is about knowing God—with an emphasis on the deep devotional lifestyle in the secret place and all aspects of prayer. She and Peter, her husband of over 30 years, reside in the San Francisco Bay area, and have one son, Kenon, who is a minister in his own right.

Pat serves on numerous boards and committees, including the International Board of Directors for Aglow International, the Covering Board of Pray the Bay, which helps to network pastors and intercessors of the San Francisco Bay area, the Facilitation Committee of Mission America, the National Prayer Committee, and the International Reconciliation Coalition (IRC). She has written an instructive prayer and fasting booklet, **Necessary Food**, and contributed a chapter to the book, **Women of Prayer, Released to the Nations** by Aglow Publications. She also publishes FLMI newsletter, "Deep Calls to Deep." She has written articles for **Charisma, Ministries Today**, and the new magazine, **Spirit Led Woman**, for which she serves on the Editorial Advisory Board. She also has written her first book, **Intimacy With the Beloved**, published by Creation House.

Chapter 3

Preparing for the Glory

Pat Chen

As I was seeking the Lord concerning this chapter, I asked Him what was it that He wanted it to express about His glory. After all, this subject is all about Him. Some of the thoughts the Lord spoke to mind included the following: There is no glory without *sacrifice*; there is no glory without *suffering*; there is no glory without *death*—not only the death that takes us into the life to come but also death to self in this life. Experiencing the glory of God will bring you into a more intimate walk with Christ. Likewise, the more intimate your walk with Christ, the more glory will come. (I have expounded on thoughts such as these in my new book, *Intimacy with the Beloved.*[1])

There are some people who want the glory of God without first paying the price of suffering. We must be willing to follow after God at any cost. I want to emphasize the importance of having a *willing* heart, because at times God's glory is revealed without any

---

1. Creation House, 1999.

requirements at all; He comes and shows who He is just because He is. At other times, a great price is required. But whatever it takes, by God's grace and help, I desire to do—in order to experience His glory in an ever-increasing manner. I feel this way because I'm on a quest, a quest for His glory.

I've been on this quest for as long as I can remember. Even as a little child, I remember that I searched, going from one church sanctuary to another, hoping to see, feel, or touch God and His Presence. I can remember, as a child, falling asleep many times after praying in the night hours, trying to communicate and have a relationship with a God I could not see. Now, looking back, I realize that what I really wanted was to experience the glory of God. Little did I know that God was in a very hot pursuit after me, much more so than I was after Him. However, His way of wooing was to allow me to first travel on my own journey, in my own way, until I became extremely hungry, thirsty, tired, and desperate for Him and His Presence. The Lord's desire was to then take me on His journey, in His way, the way of the Holy Spirit for His glory.

I am a "questant." That is, I am one who has questions and seeks answers, one who aspires to know God and the secrets of His heart. When you are on a spiritual quest, you are on an adventure with the God of all creation and there is never a dull moment. Now, after many years, some of my questions have been answered. However, others are yet to be answered according to His time. Still others will be answered when I finally see Him, face-to-face, in glory. None of us have all the answers to life's questions, or for that matter, Heaven's. However, my most major and important search for the One who has all the answers is over. All the answers to my questions are in Jesus. He knows all and is all. Jesus is my very life and breath. It is in Jesus, my Beloved, that I live, move, and have my very being (see Acts 17:28).

Now, here is the big question: What is the glory of God? Only the infinite God Himself can answer that question. And we, His finite ones, can only answer this and understand His glory to the degree that He chooses to reveal the answers to us. The answers come through a revelation of His Word and through life's experience. An understanding of God's glory comes by the help and grace of His Holy Spirit. It is given in His providential will and timing to us both individually and corporately.

Strong's Concordance gives the Hebrew definition of *glory* as expressed in Exodus 33:18 and Isaiah 6:3 as, "Weight; but only fig. In a good sense, splendor or copiousness, glorious(ly), glory, honour (able)."[2]

The glory of God is and represents the sum total of the very essence and nature of God's character and personality. His glory represents His Presence and His power. It is all of who He is and has to give. I have come to this conclusion after studying the endless definitions of the word *glory* in different reference books and other teachings. There is no way to completely and thoroughly explain the glory of God. We will be learning about it throughout all eternity.

God's glory is a manifestation of His nature and His intrinsic worth. God's glory reveals His real, genuine nature and the character of His most inward being. God's glory is the true essence of the core of who He is. His *weight* represents the heaviness of His worthiness, awesomeness, and His influence, power, and authority. *Splendor* represents His impressiveness, great brightness, and "splendor of victory." *Copiousness* represents His overwhelming abundance and fullness of supply. *Honor* represents His official dignity and reputation. Therefore, God's glory most fully boasts of His own personage, equipage, and reputation. So, if any of us would even have a small glimpse of His glory, how could we not but fall on our faces to worship, adore, and praise His holy name? How could we not help but be compelled to exalt, respect, and revere Him?

God is God. He is God all by Himself. He does not depend on anything or anybody else to make Him God.

When God's glory is being revealed, we become witnesses of His grace, goodness, faithfulness, kindness, truthfulness, holiness,

---

2. James Strong, *Strong's Exhaustive Concordance of the Bible* (Peabody, Massachusetts: Hendrickson Publishers, n.d.), glory, #H3519.

righteousness, justice, gentleness, fierceness, wrath, love, deity, presence, purity, perfection, power, authority, knowledge, wisdom, and more—which are all encompassed into one big word, *glory*. Glory, hallelujah!

Moses was not able to constantly see the glory of God on any given occasion because at times God conceals His glory. God's glory represents His sovereignty. He has Kingship over His own existence. He is in control. He governs Himself. He rules and reigns the universe and the affairs of man!

When your temple is empty, God can take it over. When you are emptied out, God can take possession of it. God fills up empty, imperfect vessels with His perfection—that is, His glory. The Scripture speaks of Christ in us, the hope of glory:

That is, the mystery which has been hidden from the past ages and generations; but has now been manifested to His saints, to whom God willed to make known what is the riches of the glory of this mystery among the Gentiles, which is Christ in you, the hope of glory (Colossians 1:26-27 NAS).

He fills us up with Himself. We become carriers of His glory.

Everyone who is called by My name, and whom I have created for My glory, whom I have formed, even whom I have made (Isaiah 43:7 NAS).

The very nature of the Lord's Presence brings conviction and cleansing. You are confronted with the Spirit of truth in His glory. An example of this is in the life of the prophet Isaiah. His encounter with the glory of God affected him to such an extent that he wailed with great lament, "Woe is me, for I am ruined! Because I am a man of unclean lips, and I live among a people of unclean lips; for my eyes have seen the King, the Lord of hosts" (Is. 6:5 NAS). If we were proper carriers of His glory, there would be more accounts of people being convicted of sin, falling on their knees, and crying out in repentance to God for forgiveness when they come into our presence. And we, too, would come under great conviction and respond as Isaiah.

The glory of God is the evidence of His Presence and has nothing to do with the nature of man. Instead, it has everything to do with the nature and attributes of God alone. You cannot project the nature of man into the nature of God because it is totally the opposite of God's pure and perfect nature. The glory of God reveals His resurrection power, energy, and pure life, and once you've experienced it, it actually makes life worth living. When you see Christ and His glory, you come to understand He is a giver, the giver of life. That is His nature. Everything that comes from His life has fruitfulness and productivity.

God chooses to reveal His glory to the corporate Body even when we don't believe and accept the reality of His glory. At times, we put God in a box and expect Him to reveal His glory in our way. Then He chooses to reveal His glory when we are totally unprepared to receive it because of our own narrow, limited thinking. We run Him away and totally close Him out when we don't mean to. There are times when we have waited and waited until His glory seems to be overdue. Then just when we least expect it, He surprises us and reveals His glory. Who can explain God and all He does?

When Solomon dedicated the temple, the Lord chose to reveal Himself to the masses. But He doesn't always reveal His glory to a large group. There are times when God chooses to reveal His glory to a single individual. Just think about all the times that the Almighty revealed His glory to Moses. What a real privilege and honor it must have been for Moses to have God come to him alone. Father God trusted Moses enough to show Himself to him privately. Some would ask, "Which is more important or better—to experience the glory of God in the crowd or alone?" I would say that it's best to experience God's glory whenever and however He chooses to reveal it. He is God, and He is sovereign. Besides, you never know when He will choose to come to you again.

God so loves to reveal Himself in a private and hidden manner. I believe that in these times the Lord is expressing to the individual the preciousness of private time together with Him. When God shows Himself to the larger corporate Body, then this encounter is no longer a secret reward. All share in it. The Creator of the universe wants to manifest and show Himself to those whom He created for Himself in a very personal way. At other times, He prefers to manifest His glorious magnificence to the masses. Personally, I feel that it is the most precious privilege to have a personal and secret touch from God, but I also appreciate His coming in splendor and glory in the midst of tons of people. Who is to know when He will come? Perhaps He will come to you today. Be ready.

How are we made ready? I believe that we are made ready when we have an open and hungry heart for a greater revelation of Jesus. We need to position ourselves for the coming of His glory. Who knows how quickly the great awakening, renewal, and revival that we have been praying for will come. Though more souls have already come into the Kingdom in our day than any other time in history, I believe we, the Body of Christ, His Bride, are still in the preparation stage and waiting for the greater manifestation of the glory of God. We are yet to have our debut before the world. We are waiting for the sons of God to be revealed to all the world (see Rom. 8:19). Who are the sons of God? We *are*. I believe that is why we all are going through so many trials and testings; we are being positioned to display more of His glory to the world.

Something is going on in the heavenlies in our day. Do you not sense this? In the next few years, His glory will be revealed, but not without a great price to the believer. So who's to know when He will come? Those who have an open and hungry heart must be ready to see, feel, and touch!

Jesus had to be properly positioned to operate in the Father's glory. His positioning was in the desert, the wilderness, and dry and barren places. Our positioning will occur in the barren places as well. Jesus had to be tempted by the enemy before He entered His public ministry, and most assuredly, we will too. Before we go to our next level of ministry, we will go through a higher testing process. We will be experiencing temptations similar to what Jesus did in the wilderness in Luke 4. Because Jesus had to go through trying and positioning, we will too.

> *And the devil said to Him, "If You are the Son of God, tell this stone to become bread." And Jesus answered him, "It is written, 'MAN SHALL NOT LIVE ON BREAD ALONE'"* (Luke 4:3-4 NAS).

We are in the days of being more properly suited and prepared for our public ministry so that His glory may be revealed in us. When nothing of this world satisfies us, we will have more depth. We will not be caught up with what will pass away. While in the desert for 40 days, Jesus had to remind the enemy what His bread was. What is our bread? Is it to do the will of the Father and fulfill His word, in spite of every inconvenience, uncomfortable circumstance, and sacrifice? When that is our meat, His glory will be revealed in us. One of the expressions of His glory is to be food for the hungry, because we are to be the broken bread and the poured-out wine for the needy.

> *And he led Him up and showed Him all the kingdoms of the world in a moment of time. And the devil said to Him, "I will give You all this domain and its glory; for it has been handed over to me, and I give it to whomever I wish* (Luke 4:5-6 NAS).

There is a glory of the world and there is the glory of God. Sometimes, we've not been able to distinguish between the two. Some of us mistake the glory of God with the glory of man. Some of us are caught up in our own glory—honor, praise, and worship of ourselves. So there is no room for His glory to be seen. There is a glory that is counterfeit. In our services and our coming together, we may conjure up our own glory. Therefore, we have strange fire because we were too impatient to wait for the real thing (see Lev. 10:1). We have been too pleased and satisfied with our own creation, the imitation.

The world's form of glory stimulates and motivates us to compete, control, and strive to be higher than others. We desire to receive the accolades and glory from man; whereas, the genuine glory invokes and mandates that we bow low and recognize our own unworthiness and nothingness. Then the Lord will receive all the attention and focus. We will, in all humility, delight in the Lord receiving all the attention and give Him all the praise! May we serve Him only, be willing to do what He wants us to do, and not serve ourselves.

And Jesus answered and said to him, "It is written, 'YOU SHALL WORSHIP THE LORD YOUR GOD AND SERVE HIM ONLY' " (Luke 4:8 NAS).

Until we worship and serve Him only, we will not see, handle, and carry His glory to the level that He so desires for us. We have been doing public ministry, but we have not always been *ready* to do so. May we handle the things of God appropriately by the principles of the Word in our public ministry.

And he led Him to Jerusalem and had Him stand on the pinnacle of the temple, and said to Him, "If You are the Son of God, throw Yourself down from here; for it is written, 'HE WILL GIVE HIS ANGELS CHARGE CONCERNING YOU TO GUARD YOU,' and, 'ON their HANDS THEY WILL BEAR YOU UP, LEST YOU STRIKE YOUR FOOT AGAINST A STONE' " (Luke 4:9-11 NAS).

One of the greatest detriments to the glory of God in the Body of Christ is to place leaders or anyone on a pedestal. The enemy deceives us, and we put each other on a pinnacle where we worship each other's talents, gifts, and personalities instead of the personhood of our Lord Jesus Christ. We don't know the Lord's tolerance level and when He will decide to flick someone off the pinnacle with His finger. Then another may foolishly climb up on that pedestal and say, "It's my turn, let me have my time. What's in this for me?" We don't always learn our lesson from the mistakes of others. In a way when we do this, we are challenging the Lord. We are trying to be in the place that He should be. It is like we are saying, "Who is the greatest? Can I be?"

And Jesus answered and said to him, "It is said, 'YOU SHALL NOT PUT THE LORD YOUR GOD TO THE TEST.'" ....And Jesus returned to Galilee in the power of the Spirit; and news about Him spread through all the surrounding district. And He began teaching in their synagogues and was praised by all (Luke 4:12,14-15 NAS).

We have sacrificed His glory rather than sacrificing ourselves. When we pass our tests, we will not have to promote or push ourselves forward or praise ourselves. News will spread about us. God Himself will exalt us, and other people will praise us. We will be more fit to do the ministry He has for us. When our hidden ministry to the Lord is strengthened, our public ministry will come in a higher form. We will be praised of men because the glory of God rests upon us and not upon anything of ourselves. Without compromise, we will declare very clearly who Jesus is and what His Word says. We will be trusted by God to carry and display His glory, proclaiming the year of the Lord. We will not be displaying our own wares, but we will be displaying His glory instead. That's why we exist.

May we humbly say what is written in Luke 4:18-19 (NAS):

"THE SPIRIT OF THE LORD IS UPON ME, BECAUSE HE ANOINTED ME TO PREACH THE GOSPEL TO THE POOR. HE HAS SENT ME TO PROCLAIM RELEASE TO THE CAPTIVES, AND RECOVERY OF SIGHT TO THE BLIND, TO SET FREE THOSE WHO ARE DOWNTRODDEN, TO PROCLAIM THE FAVORABLE YEAR OF THE LORD."

This is the way of Jesus, full of authority and power—as He Himself declared: "...Today this Scripture has been fulfilled in your hearing" (Lk. 4:21 NAS). My prayer is that this Scripture be fulfilled in us today.

37

Stephen

We will better understand the purpose and meaning of His resurrection life when we experience suffering and death to self. Acts 7:55-56 (NAS) talks of Stephen,

> *But being full of the Holy Spirit, he gazed intently into heaven and saw the glory of God, and Jesus standing at the right hand of God; and he said, "Behold, I see the heavens opened up and the Son of Man standing at the right hand of God."*

Stephen was a carrier of the glory of God. Are you a carrier of His glory too? Stephen experienced all the different dimensions of the glory of God in his life and his death. He knew how to carry the glory of God without touching it, receiving credit for it, or exploiting it (see Is. 48:11). Stephen exemplified the nature of Christ and His resurrection power even in his death. The glory of God was displayed in a revelation of Christ's resurrection power on the day that Stephen was stoned and martyred. How about you, have you been stoned lately? God may allow even your friends to cast the stones. Rest assured that even in the midst of such situations the glory of God is being formed and revealed in you for the purpose and good of others.

The definition of Stephen's name is a wonderful discovery. Strong's definition is, "to twine or wreathe; a chaplet (as a badge of royalty, a prize in the public gain or a symbol of honor gen.; but more conspicuous or elaborate than the simple fillet, 1238 [which is diadem, as bound about the head]), lit. or fig.:—crown."[3] Stephen was the first Christian martyr who died at the Eastern Damascus gate of Jerusalem. It was thought to be the site of Christ's crucifixion. In another reference, Stephen's name is shown to mean a "crown of glory." I want my crown.

Stephen experienced the glory of God and was appropriately named for the life that he lived for Christ and for the life that he died

---

3. *Strong's Concordance*, Stephen, #G4736/G4735.

in Christ. Stephen knew the God of glory intimately and became the Lord's witness. It's interesting to also note that Scripture says when he died, he had a face like that of an angel (see Acts 6:15). He maintained an innocence and guilelessness even while being stoned. In spite of the persecution, rejection, slander, false witnesses, trials, testings, and physical and spiritual abuse, he maintained the character of Christ and spoke the Word of God and truth. The intimate walk with God will empower you to go through anything.

I believe the reason that Stephen was able to gaze intently into Heaven and see Jesus at the right hand of God at his trial was because Stephen walked intimately in heavenly places while still here on earth. He knew about the highway to Heaven and how to get there. He had probably taken many spiritual journeys there before. Stephen fulfilled his purpose in his life and his death. May we each fulfill our purpose as well. How I desire to fulfill mine. I'm aspiring to see my beloved King in His entire splendor and glory. I'm on a quest, a quest for His glory.

Jesus' reputation came mostly after His death, but while He was physically walking here on the earth, He demonstrated the reputation of the Father. Jesus always pointed the people to His heavenly Father. All that Jesus was and everything He did was to the glory of His Father. Jesus carried the presence, the power, and the authority of God within Him. He carried the Father's glory in an earthly body, but the focus was upon what He was carrying and not upon His humanity.

And the Word became flesh, and dwelt among us, and we beheld His glory, glory as of the only begotten from the Father, full of grace and truth (John 1:14 NAS).

We beheld what He contained, what was in Him, and what He carried. We need to be carriers of His glory as well, with the attention directed on Him and not on us and our reputation. The glory of God is His reputation.

For we do not preach ourselves but Christ Jesus as Lord, and ourselves as your bond-servants for Jesus' sake. For

God, who said, "Light shall shine out of darkness," is the One who has shone in our hearts to give the light of the knowledge of the glory of God in the face of Christ. But we have this treasure in earthen vessels, that the surpassing greatness of the power may be of God and not from ourselves (2 Corinthians 4:5-7 NAS).

Christ's glory has been revealed from the foundation of the earth and is being revealed in us. It is so amazing that God's glory can be found in ordinary, earthen vessels such as you and me.

But we all, with unveiled face beholding as in a mirror the glory of the Lord, are being transformed into the same image from glory to glory, just as from the Lord, the Spirit (2 Corinthians 3:18 NAS).

That is, the mystery which has been hidden from the past ages and generations; but has now been manifested to His saints, to whom God willed to make known what is the riches of the glory of this mystery among the Gentiles, which is Christ in you, the hope of glory (Colossians 1:26-27 NAS).

Psalm 19:1 (NAS) says, "The heavens are telling of the glory of God...." His reputation will be preserved!

A dynamic preacher, minister, and gospel soloist, Varle Rollins is known for her sensitivity to the messages she presents in word and song. This sensitivity stems from her deep passion to see the Body of Christ come into their God-given purpose. God directs that passion to bring healing and restoration to today's families—especially women. She believes in making a demand on the deposit of unique giftings that God has placed within each individual. Varle views worship as a lifestyle, believing that everything said and done should bring honor and glory to God. She states, "There is no true anointed ministry to change lives if there is no overflow from being in the Presence of God daily."

Chapter 4

Quest for the Glory

Varle Rollins

He who dwells in the shelter of the Most High will rest in the shadow of the Almighty....If you make the Most High your dwelling—even the Lord, who is my refuge—then no harm will befall you, no disaster will come near your tent. For He will command His angels concerning you to guard you in all your ways; they will lift you up in their hands, so that you will not strike your foot against a stone. You will tread upon the lion and the cobra; you will trample the great lion and the serpent. "Because he loves Me," says the Lord, "I will rescue him; I will protect him, for he acknowledges My name" (Psalm 91:1,9-14).

I have often wondered why I seem to live in a perpetual state of curiosity about the things of God. Even as a child, I would stare at preachers and other people I thought were really close to Him, carefully studying and trying to learn from them. I was always intrigued by fiery preachers, who not only captivated my attention, but also affected me emotionally. This fascination did not mean, however, that I had any desire for public speaking. I realize now that this childhood curiosity was the beginning of a journey that eventually would draw me into the greatest move of God ever known to man.

Thus far, my journey has led me through many things usually dismissed as ordinary challenges of life, but my greatest challenges have stirred in me a desperate desire for God. They have drawn me into a continuing quest. I am amazed constantly by the incredible experiences I enjoy while seeking Him, and I am overwhelmed to realize that, while I am on a quest for God, He is and always has been on a quest for me.

In the following pages, I will share with you some of my personal encounters with God. I pray that He will reveal to you the longing that He has kindled in each of us for His Presence and that longing will fuel your own unique quest for His glory.

I was born the seventh of ten children to Edgar and Thelma Sewell. When I was 14 months old, my mother was expecting twins. So my uncle and aunt, William and Ileana Turner (my father's sister), offered to help my parents by caring for me. The Turners kept me, and they raised me as their own daughter. They became my mama and daddy in every sense. Because my father was uncomfortable with the idea of adoption, I continued to live as a "Sewell" in the Turners' home. The Turners had no other children, so I reaped the benefits of living as an only child. However, because I spent a lot of time in the home of my natural parents, I also reaped the benefits of true sibling relationships.

I now believe that God set me up. He started me on my quest by setting me apart—even as a child. My childhood was very painful at times. I developed great insecurities, fought periodic bouts of deep depression, and never knew quite where or with whom I belonged. But God had a plan for me, and He delivered me from confusion by the power of His awesome love. Looking back, I can appreciate what I might now call having enjoyed the best of both worlds: I grew up as an adopted only child in some respects, and in others, I was surrounded by a large family and learned to embrace my natural heritage. God even used my father's discomfort with adoption for my good, because the fact that I still carried the name "Sewell" grounded me firmly in my lineage. I believe that both of these familial connections uniquely implanted the quest with which God has inspired my soul.

As a little girl, I spent a lot of time with my paternal grandparents, Frank and Marjorie Sewell, who were affectionately known as "Mama House" and "Papa." Mama would go to bed early, and many nights, I was allowed to stay up with Papa. I felt a deep love for Papa. He was my best friend and one of the greatest men whom I have ever known.

Papa was a preacher, and he knew it. He would open the Bible to some favorite passage and say, "Read, child," and I would read. Then, he would turn to a hymn that he loved and say, "Sing, child," and I would sing. Papa loved to hear me sing, and I loved his responses; he always smiled and chuckled, showing that he was well pleased.

I am certain that my confidence in Papa's intensely personal, one-on-one relationship with God offered me a sense of security. When he prayed, the sound of his voice moved me so greatly that just thinking about it now raises emotions in me that I thought were long gone.

As a child, hearing of and witnessing some of Papa's experiences with God sometimes left me feeling afraid, but I know now that I was being exposed to something that birthed a holy fear within me. As I grew, a deep hunger also developed inside of me, and I was compelled on a quest to discover for myself something that I had glimpsed as a little girl. That something was the glory of God.

After I was saved, I unintentionally became self-righteous, and my arrogance hurt many. I was entrenched in religion and legalism. When I came face-to-face with my bondage, I experienced intense pain and confusion. My guilt was almost unbearable, and thoughts of suicide tormented me. Daily walks around the neighborhood were my only therapy, and many sidewalks were watered with my tears. My heart was nagged incessantly by a feeling that I had failed God. Rampant confusion stirred questions in me that could have come only from the enemy of my soul. I agonized as I heard myself say, "God cannot be real." My sanity returned only when I responded, "But God was real to Papa." This thought pushed me to the Word of God, and somehow, I kept living.

One night, when I could stand it no longer, I stood in front of my husband hysterically asking to be heard, and for the first time, I understood the need to acknowledge my anger. You see, "religion" will not allow you to admit to emotions like hatred, fear, or confusion. But I had come to know each of them well. As I shared, my husband explained to me that he loved me and was deeply sorry for my pain, but he did not know what to say. I asked him to pray for me as I went to cry out to God.

As I lay on my bed sobbing, the sound of singing began to surround me. I heard what I thought were angels' voices singing, "Jesus, Jesus, Jesus, there's just something about that name." Over and over again this song permeated the room, until I heard the Holy Spirit telling me to, "Say it. Say His name." I began to repeat, "Jesus, Jesus, Jesus."

Then, it happened—a supernatural encounter with the glory of God. As I was saying, "Jesus," I heard the sound of iron striking iron. My body was stilled. My tears vanished and were replaced by a sense of awe and security. I opened my eyes to see a dark cloud leave my body and rise to the upper corner of my bedroom. Then, I saw Jesus on the cross. Startled and somewhat paralyzed, I remembered how badly I had wanted to die. I just knew that He had come to take me home. What happened next did take me higher, but I was left here to testify of God's miraculous grace.

In my vision, I saw the gray cloud that had come out of me drawn to the cross. As I watched, that cloud moved into the body of Jesus. The sound of iron striking iron intensified, and I began to understand what I heard—the sound of a hammer driving nails into the Lord's hands and feet. As the vision began to fade, the Lord said to me, "Varle, Calvary covered all." Never before had I heard those words. I did not know these as the words of a song. At that time, I knew only that I had encountered God.

Rising from my vision, I cried tears of joy. I ran to my husband. He was shocked to see his wife, who had been hysterical moments ago and who had walked away in despair, now joyfully jumping up and down in front of him. We rejoiced together over God's lovingkindness. Soon after, the Lord gave me rest, physically and mentally, and baptized me powerfully in the Holy Spirit.

Initially, it was difficult for me to step out at church. I built defenses to protect myself from people. My insecurities threatened to consume me, but the Lord broke down every wall. Eventually, I plunged in and invested in other singers and a women's Bible study. My courage and faith were nurtured as God stretched me and showed me that He wanted to use even me to touch His people.

While leading a six-member Christian band, my spiritual discernment and insight increased. I learned to stand alone in many decisions. I really ached for God's glory in our ministry, but my pursuits were sometimes unpopular. The band was a tremendous personal outlet, as my joys, sorrows, disappointments, and fears found constant opportunity for expression.

During this season, the Lord said to me, "I have called you to lead My people into worship." Indeed, this was a BIG word. I thought that He wanted me to stand before His people and lead worship as I had seen others lead. I later learned that He intended much more.

In my early thirties, I became sick and tired of being sick and tired, so I decided to launch out on a personal quest to "find myself." Little did I understand, that to find myself, I must first lose myself (see Mt. 10:39; Jn. 12:24). The art of dying to self soon became my calling and my path to freedom.

One night at a seminar, everything changed. The speaker began to flow in the gift of knowledge. I had no sense of personal need; but without warning, I was suddenly caught up into the spiritual realm and taken out of that room. I was in what seemed to be a large, empty hospital room, stretched out on a gurney. I lay there naked, but without shame or fear. The Lord came into the room and looked at me. At the same time, I realized that He had reached His hand inside my heart and pointed to something that I had not recognized. The Great Physician had come to diagnose my true state. He spoke seven words that would change my life: "You've always felt like an unwanted child." Without any opportunity for response, I found myself back in the seminar. While I mused over my experience, I still could hear the conference speaker giving a word of knowledge. Her words caused a chill to run down my spine. She said, "A woman in this room has always felt like an unwanted child." I felt cold and hot at the same time and wept uncontrollably.

If anyone had spoken those words to me before that night, I would have thought that person was being ridiculous. God showed me, however, that deep down inside of me, a spirit of rejection had attached itself to me the day that I had left my natural parents' home to live with my aunt and uncle. My husband and I prayed together, and I knew that I must talk it all through again with my natural parents. I dreaded the moments that I was about to face, but the Lord assured me that talking to my parents would set me free.

We invited them to dinner. My chest was so tight that I thought that I would explode, but I pressed on. My father and mother could sense that this would be more than a casual evening of sharing, but their graciousness exceeded their anxiety. After dinner, I knew that it was time to share my story. With a supportive glance from my husband, I began. Everyone listened quietly. I tried not to cry, but the tears would not be stifled. I explained that I always knew and understood the story of my early life, but that God had told me to hear the story NOW from my parents.

My father overflowed with emotion as he began to tell my real story. He said that he never really wanted me to be raised by anyone else but had reluctantly chosen to receive the Turners' help.

He explained the struggle he had felt, even then, feeling as if he had given his child away.

As my father continued to share, I began to feel significance and purpose well up inside of me. He shared that when I left his home, God led him to the story of Moses. My father spoke over me that night as if he were a prophet. He said that I was special, and that he always knew that God would use me.

It is difficult to describe what I experienced. What had started as an awkward evening, ended as a night of deliverance. Feelings of liberty, safety, security, and love overwhelmed me. I had even asked why I had been named Varle (pronounced "Verl"), but after that night, it no longer mattered. The years of seeing my name misspelled, hearing it mispronounced, questioned, and ridiculed, seemed now to have happened to someone else. (Later, the Lord told me that my name means "victory" and that it is a heavenly name.) My father died one year later.

The release that began with my father that evening spilled over into my praise and worship. Finally, I was free to raise my hands. Previously, I had raised only my right hand to the Lord because I was self-conscious about a defect of my left hand. Now, I express total surrender. All self-consciousness has disappeared. Now, my left hand signifies that God had marked me for His glory from my birth. Now, being the seventh child and being named Varle are signs that God has set me apart for such a time as this.

Years later, the church that we had grown to love faced a split. My heart was broken, but we suspected that it was time for us to move on. Everything within me cried out to stay where I was to continue to care for those I loved and in whom I had invested so much. Then, one day, while waiting on the Lord, I read in Oswald Chambers' *My Utmost for His Highest*, "Obey, and leave the consequences to Me." What seemed like a hard word became evidence of God's grace, launching us into our next phase. Also, He blessed me with what later became my signature song, "He'll Do It Again."

In our new church, I was stretched to another level of leadership. As a praise and worship leader, I learned that I could not lead anyone where I had not gone myself. Pursuing the mind of the Holy Spirit became my passion until I was consumed with desire for His Presence, and I trained the team not only in music, but also in the real meaning of worship and how to be a worshiper.

Without expectation, I soon found myself traveling from state to state singing in churches and conferences. For a woman who had never traveled and knew nothing about the big world of ministry, this was overwhelming. I felt unqualified, but God used me.

To my surprise, I found myself in Arizona at a retreat for women in leadership. Sitting among women I had read and heard about, I felt totally intimidated, like a little spoke among the big wheels. That very first night I knew that my life would change forever. The message emphasized our need for God's Presence and for deeper intimacy with Him. My every longing was exposed and, at last, the deep hunger inside of me was defined. I devoured every word as if my life depended on it.

I came home with a gleam in my eye and a new song in my heart. I had stepped into another realm of glory and there was no turning back. As I shared what had happened, people looked at me as though I was speaking a foreign language. I must admit that being misunderstood frustrated me, but my hunger for more persisted. My personal times with the Lord became like stepping into a room full of intoxicating aromas; one revelation followed into another. Now when I ministered, I could feel the anointing released inside of me. The overflow came so strongly that it soon became obvious that I was called not only to sing, but also to preach.

I never received the formal training I desired, but along came the Holy Spirit to be my teacher. Over the next three years, I developed friendships with some of the women I met at the retreat and I began to grow as a minister. Never in my wildest dreams could I have imagined that I would receive such intense equipping and training. During our third retreat, I received this clarifying word: "Varle, the

Lord would say to you that it's not either/or; it's both/and." God was confirming that I would sing, preach, and manifest other gifts, and that I was not to worry about how I, as the messenger, was perceived. God would no longer allow anyone else to define my calling. He assumed total control. I lay awake all night as He saturated me with confidence. However, not everyone embraced and celebrated this prophecy. To the contrary, it brought offense. I found myself standing alone again, with my heart shattered.

When my husband and I heard the words, "Rise up, and go," we headed into the unknown. Matthew 11:28-30 and God's responses to our prayers indicated that He was calling us into a type of rest. Soon, God questioned me specifically with the piercing words, "Will you lay down your reputation, your rights, and even your life for Me?" You can only imagine how much I wanted to know what this could mean.

For the next two months, my husband and I attempted to rest. Many nights, I dreamed of worshipers sitting in a congregation as I stood behind the pulpit, preaching the Word of God. Then the Lord said, loud and clear, "I have raised you up by My own hand that I would receive the glory. Now, I am ready to release you as pastor, and you will start a church." I fearfully pondered this word and waited a few days before telling my husband. Little did I know, he also had heard from God. We were called to pastor as a team.

While visiting another church during our transition, I was worshiping as a saxophonist played "Joy of My Desire, All Consuming Fire." I pressed into the Lord's Presence and was taken away in spirit. I sat at a table in a dark room with my head in my hands as one in despair. When I noticed light coming into the room, I looked up to see a door opening in front of me. Then, Jesus stepped into view from behind the door, looked at me, and motioned for me to come outside with Him. I followed Him, and as I stepped through the door, a great, thunderous sound overwhelmed me. When I looked, I saw a powerful waterfall. I remember thinking that I was at Niagara Falls, but somehow I knew that this great waterfall was not to be named by any human. As I looked at the falls and listened to the sound, I noticed Jesus motioning for me to jump in. I hesitated because the falls had walls too high to measure, and the river seemed as wide as it was long. The moving water was very active, as if it were alive with excitement about something. The Lord motioned again for me to jump in, but I could only think of my inability to swim. As I looked at the Lord, His Presence seemed to launch me into the water. I found myself doing strokes I had seen on the Olympics. As I looked at Jesus again, He was laughing. The more He laughed, the more excited the river became. Then, I began to laugh. I realized that He was enjoying watching me as I was refreshed and overtaken with joy. I left church that day with renewed vision and purpose.

As we dove into our new calling, we prayed about what to name our church. Believing that the name of the church should be prophetic, I was reminded of my vision. As a result, Living Waters Worship Center was born.

My passion for God's Presence intensified, and His glory became almost tangible as we worshiped in our living room. Many nights, I could not remain in bed because my ears were so full of God's voice. I came into such a strong anointing so fast that it not only threw me, but it also caused me to struggle within about where I now fit into my circle of family and friends. Things changed so quickly. I did not always know how to respond when asked about why some phone calls were less frequent and others ceased. This outgoing woman had to prioritize her time. I now had a mandate: I knew that I was called to usher in a fresh move of God. I was willing to do whatever was necessary to make myself available to God. I was determined not to allow anyone or anything hinder me from seeing God's glory, but I wanted to take with me anyone who was willing to follow. Again, I was being separated, and I would soon discover just how high the cost would be.

Our living room became our church. God said that we would be a fresh model of what He is doing in the Church. Regular walks to the elementary school in our neighborhood singing, "We Are Standing on Holy Ground" proved profitable. We laid our hands on that building and began to believe that God would give it to us for our church services, and He did.

Later, while ministering at a women's conference, I was pulled to another level. Shirley Arnold was one of the guest speakers at the conference, and after she spoke, she laid hands on most of the women. I tried to focus on my responsibilities to the praise and worship team; however, it felt as though my efforts were somehow being bombarded. As Shirley passed behind me, I felt like I was caught up in a whirlwind. I started running in place uncontrollably. Then, I started to spin like a top. The catchers were suddenly faced with a new challenge called Varle Rollins. I came home from that trip and preached the most anointed and powerful message I had ever preached. I proceeded to lay hands on everyone in my living room. All were slain in the Spirit and rose later knowing that the glory of God truly had come to Living Waters Worship Center.

The closer the Holy Spirit drew me, the more He used me to draw the congregation closer by fanning the flame of their desire for Him. Leading God's people into worship as a pastor is now a reality.

I have touched something that keeps me in holy awe of God. I receive testimonies from people who have been healed or delivered through this ministry. One woman was healed of a nerve disorder in her leg when she walked past me at a conference. Regular requests for me to preach come from churches all across the country. I birthed an outreach ministry for women called Joyspring to tear down the walls that have divided us. I now mentor about 100 women monthly and host an annual conference. Miracles have permeated our congregation. My sister, who suffered from Lupus for eight years, was recently healed. One of our youth had an enlarged heart with a hole in it. He was completely healed one morning in church, which was documented in a local newspaper shortly thereafter. Our youth are on fire for God, and the youth dance troupe ministers with a powerful, yoke-breaking anointing. Most of the younger children are baptized in the Holy Spirit and love to worship. They also minister powerfully through dance.

My intention is never to bring scorn to the name of Christ or the ministry. My objective is not to glorify myself or to suggest that I should be seen as somehow special. It is my desire, however, to declare that I know with certainty the truth of Second Corinthians 4:7 (KJV)—that I have a treasure in my earthen vessel, that the excellency of the power may be of God and not of me.

My life has taken many turns, yet only one thing drives me—a burning desire to know Him. He uses each heartbreak, disappointment, and tragedy to draw me closer to Him and to press me toward my destiny. Now, I am in full-time ministry. Look what the Lord has done!

It seems that I have searched most of my life for something that I was unable to define. Many times in my quest for God's glory, I felt certain that I had lost my way; but He has promised, "If you seek Me, you will find Me" (see Jer. 29:13).

Please, join me in the journey and be encouraged by Second Corinthians 3:18 (NKJ):

But we all, with unveiled face, beholding as in a mirror the glory of the Lord, are being transformed into the same image from glory to glory, just as by the Spirit of the Lord.

From glory to glory, the quest continues…

"My driving passion is 'Christ in me, the hope of Glory,' " so stated by Dr. Flo Ellers, the founder of Global Glory Ministries, Inc. based in Juneau, Alaska. Flo attended the Institute of Ministry in Bradenton, Florida in 1982; she has her Master's of Ministry with Shalom Bible College and Seminary in West Des Moines, Iowa as well as her Doctorate of Theology with Shalom Bible College and Seminary. Flo is currently ordained under Pastor Jeff Johns of White Horse Christian Center in West Lafayette, Indiana. She is an endtime revivalist who has been traveling to the nations since 1985. She preaches the Word of God in great boldness and sees mighty signs, wonders, and miracles. Her deepest desire is to see the kingdoms of this world become the Kingdom of our God and of His Christ. Flo has been married for 37 years and has four daughters and nine grandchildren.

Chapter 5

Dancing in the Glory

Dr. Flo Ellers

A People of Praise

n the Old Testament, God inhabited the *praises* of His people (see Ps. 22:3 KJV), but in New Testament days in which we now live, God inhabits a *people* of praise (see Jn. 4:23-24). The Malaysian people are a people of praise! Revival started in Pastor Nicholas Wu's church in Kuala Lumpur in 1993. On my second trip to Malaysia after the revival began, I was teaching daytime sessions on the subject of *The Anointing.* The exhilarating praise made it easy to enter into the anointing because the people had been "soaking" in God's Presence for days. We were all so enraptured in "the glory" that it was difficult for Pastor Nick to go to the platform to introduce me. I stood behind the pulpit and looked out over the people. I could hardly see. My eyelids seemed to be "slain in the Spirit"—just my eyelids!

I announced to the congregation that I would not be laying hands on them because the same anointing that was upon me and in me dwelt in them also. While I was teaching, Pastor Nick had to leave the meeting briefly to go to his office on the lower level of the church building. I finished teaching and told the people to stand up and form groups of five. I instructed them to hold hands and ask each other what their needs were. Then I shouted for them to start praying in tongues for one another. From the moment they opened their mouths to pray, the volume of their voices was deafening. The room filled with "the glory," and they began to sway under the power of God. Suddenly, the fire fell! Boom, boom, boom! To my utter delight, the people were falling everywhere! Yes, the same anointing that was on me was now on them! Glory to God!

The place looked like a battlefield. I continued to peer through my now almost closed eyes. It was an amazing sight. Pastor Nick came through the doorway to investigate what all the noise was about. As he started down the middle aisle, he began to bend low under the weight of the glory and started to stagger toward me. He could hardly walk. He finally made it to the platform and asked me what happened. I recall saying something to this effect, "God showed up!"

As the glory lifted, a woman asked me to pray for her leg. I raised my hand toward her and began to pray, "Father, in the name of Jesus…" That was as far as I got. She threw her arms into the air and started to shake wildly. To my amazement, she was thrown to the floor and hit her head with a loud thud! By then Pastor Nick had joined us and we both watched as an invisible hand took her leg (which was vibrating violently) and turned it *completely* around. That, in the natural, is impossible to do. My mouth fell open, and my eyes opened wide in amazement. Then another hand, one more powerful than the first, took her leg and twisted it back around. She was totally healed by the power of the living God! Whoop glory!

When Will the Glory Come?

Once you have seen, tasted, and experienced the glory of God, you, like Moses of old will continue to cry out, "Lord, show me more of Your glory!" (see Ex. 33:18) Because of the cry of Moses' heart and the destiny upon his life, God called Moses to come up to the mountain to meet with Him there. When God calls you, you cannot help but go, for who can resist such a God?

During those initial 40 days on Mount Sinai, Moses was so *saturated* in the "glory" that afterward, it was visible to all who saw him. God spoke to Moses from out of the glory cloud. When we come under the glory cloud, Jesus will speak to us, too. Moses came down to the people carrying with him an exact pattern for the erecting of the tent where God would meet with him. Moses built the tent according to God's plan. Exodus 40:33b (KJV) says, "So Moses *finished* the work." Then the glory fell!

God called Solomon to build His temple in Second Chronicles 5:1 (KJV), "Thus all the work that Solomon made for the house of the Lord was *finished*...." Then the glory fell! Verse 14 (KJV) says, "...the priests could not stand to minister by reason of the cloud: for the glory of the Lord had filled the house of God." When God's glory falls, you won't be able to stand either!

"When Jesus therefore had received the vinegar, He said, It is *finished*..." (Jn. 19:30 KJV). Jesus said that when His work was completed He would go back to His Father in Heaven, but He would not leave us comfortless (see Jn. 14:17-20). He promised to send the Holy Spirit, who would not only come alongside of us to help us in our everyday activities, but would come to live inside of us. As Jesus was ascending into Heaven, He said to all 500 onlookers, "And, behold, I send the promise of My Father upon you: but tarry ye in the city of Jerusalem, until ye be endued with power from on high" (Lk. 24:49 KJV). Fifty days later only 120 "onlookers" were left in the upper room when suddenly the Holy Spirit came out of Heaven with lightning speed, splitting the sky like the rushing of a violent tempest blast and filling the whole house. Then the glory fell!

The Holy Spirit so saturated the believers that they began to speak in other languages telling of the mighty works of God! The first thing that happened when the glory fell was that an incredible boldness came upon Peter so that he began to preach *loudly*, telling the people to repent. When you come under the glory, the Lord brings joy, boldness to witness, and purity to live a life worthy of the One you represent. The Bible says that *you* are now the *temple* of God, so when He comes in and floods your being with His glory, *something is going to happen!*

The woman in Malaysia was healed after I finished bringing the message of the glory anointing that God had sent me there to deliver. When you have an assignment from God and complete it, the glory will fall!

A Little Child and the Glory

In an evening meeting in Malaysia, a woman testified that her five-year-old son and his friend had been in the morning service and had been "slain in the Spirit." After helping her son up, she asked him what had happened. He said that he was just walking among the people who were slain in the Spirit when suddenly he too went down. Then he told his mother, "I saw a big man sitting on a big chair, but I couldn't see his face. Then I saw Grandma dancing and dancing." The boy also saw his grandma's friend, although both of them had died two years earlier! The boy had been caught up into the throne room of Heaven! I believe that as the boys wandered among those on the floor, they must have stepped into a "pocket of glory," or perhaps where an angel was standing, and got "caught up" into the glory of God.

Dancing in the Glory

During another evening service, the praise and worship band was especially anointed. I got up to dance Indian-style (I am of Native American descent) when suddenly a bright light shone on me as if a 20,000-watt bulb had lit up in my face. I began waving my arm (which felt like a palm branch moving with the wind) and saying, "I am standing in the very Presence of the Lord Almighty, worshiping Him, worshiping Him, worshiping Him." I felt as though a warm breeze was blowing on me. Everything seemed to be moving in slow motion. It was glorious! The next thing I knew, I was sitting on the front row and Pastor Nick was introducing me to come and preach the Word. Immediately after the meeting, several women came to me; they were exclaiming over how suddenly and powerfully I had hit the floor. I told them, "No, I didn't!"

They said, "Yes, you did. Ask Sister Charlotte." So, I asked her. She told me that while I was dancing, I had suddenly hit the floor and had lain there for some time. Sister Charlotte said everyone had seen it. As she was relating the story to me, I mentally told the Lord that I never wanted to cross over into the glory again until He explained to me what had really happened that evening—and why I couldn't remember falling to the floor.

After coming home from Malaysia I called Rodney Howard-Browne's office. His assistant returned my phone call and listened to my story. The first thing he told me was that my experience was not a result of witchcraft. He knew of my Indian ancestry and thought I was attributing it to that. He then told me a story of a woman who was on a well-known prophet's platform who had been dancing under the power of God. As she danced with her eyes closed, she stepped off the platform into midair, turned around, danced back to the platform, and sat down. He said everyone had seen it, but that to this day the woman herself does not remember it. I felt relieved. Sometimes the natural man cannot receive the things of the Spirit (see 1 Cor. 2:14 KJV). Second Corinthians 5:13 (KJV) says, "For whether we be beside ourselves, it is to God: or whether we be sober, it is for your cause." When the Holy Spirit led me to these Scriptures I felt that I was standing on a firm foundation. Yes, I had been lost in the glory. However, I also believe that Paul knew something about it as well.

Revelation—A Result of the Glory

Now the Lord is that Spirit: and where the Spirit of the Lord is, there is liberty. But we all, with open face beholding as in a glass the glory of the Lord, are changed into the same image from glory to glory, even as by the Spirit of the Lord (2 Corinthians 3:17-18 KJV).

This passage means that we are changed from character to character into His character, and His ability. For example, when Adam was shrouded in the glory, he was empowered to name every animal by revelation.

Ephesians 1:17-18 (KJV) says, "That the God of our Lord Jesus Christ, the Father of glory, may give unto you the spirit of wisdom and revelation in the knowledge of Him: the eyes of your understanding being enlightened; that ye may *know....*" When we come under the glory, when we stay in His Presence, revelation will come. Revelation may come through the written Word, vision, or His still small voice in our spirits, but it will come.

When John G. Lake preached, he found himself saying things he had never heard or learned before. When that "glory anointing" came upon him, he would look at his secretary, who was transcribing his messages and give her a nod. She would mark the place, then write his words down. Later when she did research, she invariably found that those things that John Lake said while under the inspiration of the "glory anointing" were true! Only as John Lake remained under the glory was he granted wisdom and revelation of insight into mysteries and secrets of God. I have found that when I am under a heavy, glory anointing I can preach by revelation knowledge at times as well. When that happens, I say, "That's good preaching, Sister Flo!"

Revelation knowledge is coming back to the Church once again. When spiritual awakening hit America at the turn of the century, many inventions came out of the "glory anointing" that contributed to the birth of the industrial revolution.

God is about to reveal another aspect of Himself. The revelations of God are always progressive. He is taking us from glory to glory. There is a side of God which modern man has not yet experienced. Romans 8:17-18 from the Amplified Bible declares,

*And if we are [His] children, then we are [His] heirs also: heirs of God and fellow heirs with Christ [sharing His inheritance with Him]; only we must share His suffering if we are to share His glory. [But what of that?] For I consider that the sufferings of this present time (this present life) are not worth being compared with the glory that is about to be revealed **to us** and **in us** and **for us** and conferred **on us!***

The Glory in My Alaskan Village

There has always been a deep, abiding hunger for God in my heart. I wanted to know Him even as a child. Before the outbreak of revival came to our little village of Klawock on Prince of Wales Island in southeastern Alaska, there was much drunkenness among our people; but when revival came, that all changed.

One day in 1954, my Grandmother Elizabeth told us that some missionaries had come to our Indian village. We all went to the meetings they were holding in the town hall. It was there that I first heard about *Dee Kee on Kow*, "The Rich Man from above" (in my Tlingit language) and *Dee Kee on Kow do Yeet*, "The Rich Man's Son." The missionary couple, Leroy and Grace Hensyel, had been sent by the Lord to bring salvation to my people.

Grace Hensyel tells of the vision that brought her to us in her book on the Alaskan Revival entitled *God Is a Purse Maker*. The book begins:

"My rebellious head had no more than touched the pillow when a most unusual thing happened to me. In vision I was transported to Alaska, but time had rolled back more than one hundred years. I was spectator to a scene being enacted on an island in the waters of the Pacific off the coast of Alaska ... The scene on that island that unfolded before my startled eyes, is far too great for me to write in its entirety."[1]

---

1. Grace Hensyel, *God Is a Purse Maker* (Columbus, GA: Brentwood Christian Press, 1992), 11

That vision brought Grace to our people in 1954. Soon after she arrived, the Lord Jesus visited our village of 500 Indians with mighty signs, wonders, and miracles through this godly woman's yielded life. The dead were raised back to life. Oil appeared on people's hands and on their outer garments. Two-year-old children prophesied. The little bottle of anointing oil which many sick were anointed with never went dry during the three-year revival. Tongues of fire were seen by the saved and unsaved alike. Almost everyone in the village saw the Fire of God. Grace Hensyel recounts the story:

"In the Fisherman's Club that night, the service had been outstanding! God was there in a special way and as usual, people were reluctant to leave. The village light plant died, pounding out its last kilowatt of energy for the day. The gasoline lantern had gulped its final drop of fluid and sputtered out. Yet the people lingered. Out came the flashlights to guide us toward the Elmore house where we were living while our new church was in process of being built. As we were ready to leave the building, a strange light appeared over the pulpit. It was a beautiful bluish white. We watched in amazement as it moved towards a window near the pulpit. Then it was outside and moving toward our new church building. In shocked silence we watched as that strange ball of fire touched the roof of our unfinished church and then moved on to the Smith's house where it hovered for a few seconds. Then to the Roberts' home and on throughout the village. We noticed that the wonderful light only stopped over the homes of those who had received the infilling of the Spirit. We all watched in amazement, the ball of fire going before us as we walked home. Every eye was upon it, held in rapt fascination. Then it was over our home. I became horrified as seemingly fire spread over our entire roof. As the flames leaped, I cried out, "God help us, the house is burning and it isn't ours!" As we watched in stunned wonder, the flames gathered into one place and I declare that what appeared to be a band of angels, in glistening white, slowly raised from our roof and disappeared into the heavens. We all remained speechless as each departed for his own home, thinking his own silent thoughts."[2]

From that visitation in our village, revival fire was birthed in me, and I have never been the same. In 1994, 40 years after that outpouring, I went back to Prince of Wales Island and held revival services. Sister Hensyel's daughter, Judy, came to our services. She and her husband, George, were our musicians for the night. The revival spirit rested also on Judy. She began to play the piano; George played his guitar. All of a sudden the atmosphere changed, and the glory came rolling in! While Judy was playing, some papers dropped from the piano. Judy bent over to pick them up, but the *piano kept playing*! The angels didn't miss a beat or a note! George saw what happened and started bounding across the room, guitar in hand like Chuck Berry. We all started whooping and hollering and shouting and dancing, including my 70-year-old Uncle Theodore.

The glory cloud hit the youth, and they fell to the floor, rolling and laughing uncontrollably. When the power of God hit one young woman, her face turned red with fire. She could not speak English for hours; the glory cloud was so thick!

At midnight, the pastor decided to shut down the meeting. He went to the pulpit and struck his guitar strings three times, but no sound came. He was dumbfounded. Then he realized he could not speak. After several minutes in God's Presence, he was finally able to open his mouth. He said that he had never been unable to speak before. Once you are touched by revival fire, you will never be quite the same. You will be a carrier of the revival spirit!

In this hour of the glory in the Church, Jesus will show Himself for who He is—fire from the loins down and fire from the loins up! Our God is a consuming fire (see Heb. 12:29). The world is about to experience it! His cloud of glory and pillar of fire will literally be

---

2.   *Ibid.*, 78-79.

seen by all mankind in the coming days. Just as when Moses went up into Mount Sinai, "And the glory of the Lord abode upon mount Sinai....And the sight of the glory of the Lord was like devouring fire..." (Ex. 24:16-17 KJV), so shall this fire be seen once more upon His people.

CNN and newspapers will report, "*Awesome Tongues of Fire Seen on Local Church and a Strange Cloud Descends on Entire City*" ... "*People Falling Down Everywhere!*" As Isaiah prophesied, "And the glory of the Lord shall be revealed, and all flesh shall see it together: for the mouth of the Lord hath spoken it" (Is. 40:5 KJV).

The Glory and Miracles

Whenever we see "the glory" mentioned in the Bible, it is connected with miracles. Isaiah the prophet said in Isaiah 35:2,5 (KJV), "It shall blossom abundantly...the *glory* of Lebanon shall be given.... *Then* the eyes of the blind shall be opened, and the ears of the deaf shall be unstopped." Wherever God shows up and is allowed to have His way, miracles happen.

Since 1989, I have seen mighty miracles everywhere that I have traveled in the nations. I have literally seen the glory cloud over a meeting. I have felt His literal wind blowing. I have seen His fire fall, but not to the degree that we *shall* see and experience. This latter glory is increasing in every nation and in every city that is open to Him and in every hungry heart that is crying out for more.

The Lord Jesus has put the desire in our hearts to see more of His glory because He wants to bring in the final harvest of souls. When His glory falls, miracles happen. Miracles validate the gospel. Miracles prove that we serve a powerful and living God. Cry out for the gift of miracles. Someone may say, "Aren't we supposed to seek the Giver, rather than the gifts?" My Bible says, "Earnestly desire and cultivate the spiritual gifts" (1 Cor. 14:1b AMP). Go ahead and ask the Father in Jesus' name for the gifts of the Holy Spirit. Ask Him. It's your Pentecostal inheritance (see Acts 2). Say, "*Lord Jesus, I ask You to flood me right now with Your Presence. Use me like You have never used me before. Let Your glory fall on me. I want to receive all that You have for me. Oh, thank You, Jesus. Thank You."*

The Glory and His Abundance

This present glory is connected with abundance. The first time that *glory* is mentioned in Scripture is Genesis 31:1. It has to do with material substance, or the riches of God. Money cometh! The transference of wealth came to the children of Israel as they were about to enter into the promised land. As spiritual Israel, the Church is about to enter into its promised land. The Lord will give an abundance of revelation, an abundance of anointing for creative miracles, and abundance of wealth in this hour to get the gospel out! God will bring an abundance of Christ's rich character to convince the world that He is a very good God. He will show the world His goodness and kindness by drawing a line of division between His people and the people of the world. His mark will be upon His people; they will be a people of distinction. Divine favor will come upon them: That *chabod*, or "weightiness of God's glory," will give the Church the advantage (the weight) to tip the scales in favor of God's Kingdom.

There is a sleeping giant arising. It is the Church without spot or wrinkle that will walk in the *same measure* of anointing that Jesus walked in (see Jn. 14:12). Each one will flow in his gifting as the Holy Spirit leads him in these final, most glorious hours of the Church.

Be calm, cool, and steady. Accept every hardship unflinchingly as you fulfill your destiny. Each one of us has a small part to do—and only a small part. Yet when we stand before His throne and give an account of our ministry while on earth, let us join with our elder brother Jesus and say, "It is *finished*" (see Jn. 17:4; 19:30). Let us join with our brother Paul in declaring, "I have fought the good fight, I have *finished* the race..." (2 Tim. 4:7).

Of all the signs and wonders I have seen—the fire, the glory cloud, the wind, the oil—and all the miracles, nothing could ever be compared to seeing His wonderful face and hearing Him say to me, "Well done, Daughter." All the battles, all the scars, all the victories, and, yes, all the failures are worth it in my quest for His glory!

Sue Ahn is a woman with a heart that beats for the Kingdom of God and a passion for Jesus. She longs for every human being to realize that there is no greater life-transforming power than the revelation of the love of God and for each one to become His child. Most often found serving or caring for children and teens in the background, Sue has a rich word and an anointing to impart the goodness and love of God and His faithfulness to keep His promises. Sue is the wife of international minister Dr. Ché Ahn of Harvest Rock Church and Harvest International Ministries based in Pasadena, California. Together, she and her husband have pastored more than 20 years. They have four teenage children, Gabriel, Grace, Joy, and Mary.

Chapter 6

Touching Heaven, Changing Earth

Sue Ahn

"Think of yourself as one about to take a journey. Like all expeditions, our journey starts with a departure. Long before we ever arrive at holiness, we must depart from self-righteousness and pride. If we would live in the presence of God, we must first travel the way of humility and truth. ... In our desire to know God, we must discern this about the Almighty: He resists the proud but His grace is drawn to the humble. Humility brings grace to our need, and grace alone can change our hearts. Humility is the essence of all virtues."[1]

his is how my personal quest for God's glory began...with the *truth*. The truth was that my marriage was in broken pieces. My drifting marriage of 15 years was built on a weak

1.   Francis Frangipane, *Holiness, Truth and the Presence of God* (Cedar Rapids, Iowa: Arrow Publications, 1986), 7, 10.

foundation. Damaging cracks were exposed. My husband and I desperately needed a touch of God from Heaven to change our earthly circumstances. Thus began a journey, a quest, starting with my departure from the fear of man through doing things "right" yet denying the truth of transparency and need. Reading and hearing the evidence of a spiritual renewal coming to the Body of Christ brought me hope that things might change.

It was 1994. I began to hear about miracles of glory (the tangible Presence of God) taking place in various locations around the earth. Testimonies of inner and physical healings documented the spiritual phenomenon flowing from Toronto, Canada, with Pastors John and Carol Arnott. I thought, *Perhaps there is a miracle for me; perhaps something will happen for me. Maybe the glory of God will heal my broken heart and my broken marriage.* I was desperate for God.

I yearned for the glory of God to come into the brokenness. I wanted Psalm 63 to be a reality for us as a couple, that somehow in the barren areas of our marriage Jesus would be glorified. It was the cry of my hurting heart. The Lord was faithful to answer my prayers. I took a closer look into myself and my marriage as a recording of my life was rewound:

Ché and I met while helping out after a Tuesday evening Bible study that had gathered weekly in Washington, D.C. in 1986. Ché was 22 and I was 23 when we married. (I had become a born-again Christian two years earlier.) On September 2, one day following our wedding, Ché was ordained as a pastor. Our third month anniversary brought the blessed discovery of our first pregnancy. Facing these new changes revealed a huge identity crisis. Busyness occupied our time: Doing good, Christian faith deeds justified that we had a good marriage, a good family, and a good ministry. Anyone observing outwardly would have said that everything in our lives was just great, and it was, in a sense, except for one thing—we lacked the reality of completeness and unity of true intimacy.

There remained an intangible void in both of us that we were unable to know. There was a mutual, unknown, deep barrier that protected childhood wounds of fear, confusion, misunderstanding, and loneliness, problems that remained ignorantly uncared for and unaddressed in our marriage. Insecurities surfaced in each of us, as neither of us knew how to confront the pain. The significance and affirmation I so desperately needed from Ché as my husband remained unrealized. Uncovered and vulnerable, the only place I could find the security, protection, and worth I longed for was by running like a child into the arms of God. The quest for His glory in my life began with my desperate need for the revelation of the Father's love.

It caused me to humble myself. By His mercy and incredible love, I received more than I ever asked, dreamed, and prayed for. Becoming like a child, completely trusting and dependent upon my heavenly Father, brought rest, safety, and security. Little children are completely trusting and dependent; they are without doubt or unbelief, quick to forgive, and ultimately receptive and dependent upon every leading, decision, and provision that their parents choose. No wonder the glory of God is revealed to small children and the Kingdom of God belongs to such as these. It is when we arrive at the end of ourselves, empty and broken, that the glory of God can meet us. How wise is our Father to esteem with extravagant worth and value that which the world despises as weak, useless, unimportant, and insignificant!

The measure with which we humble ourselves as a little child is the same measure with which we accept and esteem the grace to become as we are to God. This acceptance allows the glory of God to dwell in our lives. As we decrease, God increases. Jesus Christ then is exalted among the people and places we influence: our homes, schools, workplaces, neighborhoods, marriages, families, and relationships. The glory of God, the manifest Presence of God, residing within a human life is powerfully impacting. Yet He chooses to place Himself in us—imperfect, frail vessels—transforming our lives into trophies of His love. When Heaven touches earth, remarkable changes take place. The glory of God in each of us has the super-natural, life-giving power to penetrate and heal the desolate places of the soul and to touch and revive every dead region of the earth!

Be exalted, O God, above the heavens, and let your glory be over all the earth (Psalm 108:5).

We need His glory to arise. There are tombs of death within every human heart. God desires to call forth the Lazarus in us all so we may take off the grave clothes and exchange them for the glory of the living God. Humility is the door for the actualized Presence of God to permeate those places of death. God showed me the dead tomb of my marriage where He desired to resurrect life in His glory. He invited me through the door of humility one night in the spring of 1996.

The Visitation

The words were still fresh in my heart as I returned home from the evening church service. The sweetness of the a cappella melody resounded in my head, "Let Your glory fall in this place; let it flow forth from here to the nations...." It had been a wonderful time of worshiping, praying, and seeking God's face together with a small group of desperate people at John R. Mott Auditorium in Pasadena, California, the place where Harvest Rock Church meets. Now home, I washed the remaining dishes of the day, wiped off counter tops, and cleaned the floor. It was Saturday night at 11:15. Suddenly, a loud rumbling of feet, voices of heavenly tongues, and words of Scripture began to spring forth rapturously from the other room. My daughter Joy and her friend Christine had been camping out there on the floor in sleeping bags. Apparently, God had other plans for what had originally been conceived as a 12-year-old's sleepover.

Stepping into that room proved to be entering a realm not of this world. As I entered, all three of us shook violently as if a Benev-olent Being took over by loving surprise. Unusual, unrecognizable sounds filled the air of that plain room. Touching one another only intensified this violent intruder. It was as if raw voltage went

74

through our bodies on contact. My first thought was, *Oh my God! This must be like the day of Pentecost! God is with us!*

Suddenly a sound like the blowing of a violent wind came from heaven and filled the whole house where they were sitting (Acts 2:2).

Then, simultaneously, Joy and Christine both shouted, "Mott, we must go to Mott (Auditorium). Angels are there. God is coming! Souls! Souls! Mott is too small. There are flames of fire, flying doves, angels, so many angels of so many sizes. We must go!" It was a pure, childlike edict that pierced through me. It was a call to a divine appointment with God!

I gathered the two girls and my other two daughters, and we quickly drove to Mott. Entering the auditorium, part of an old Nazarene college facility, we immediately beheld a thick cloud resting all about the dim sanctuary. A lush fragrance filled the air. A realm of Heaven was open before us as we stood there in the midnight silence at the threshold of God's glory. I was awestruck as I heard the girls describing in unison the dimension that they were seeing.

There were doves, tongues of fire, and a myriad of angelic hosts worshiping from every seat with a beautiful, unfamiliar heavenly sound. The invisible was made visible. Heaven was touching earth and God was changing us in His glory on that one simple night. It was a night to forever remember!

My personal revelation of the glory of God on that calm night as He inhabited Mott was the deepest, most dramatic revelation of God that I have ever experienced. Since that time, no other time with the living God has compared. All I could do was weep uncontrollably, prostrated in praise and worship, as at the center of the large sanctuary, a thick, white cloud of pure, unending heavenly worship flowed in a sacred, vertical chasm from Heaven. It reached and touched that space of floor on earth at Mott.

My human understanding could not contain the holiness of His beauty and His all-embracing peacefulness that swallowed my entire being. In the Presence of God's holy glory, there became a clear distinction between His absolute purity and my desperate human need for Him. The great outpouring of love from my Father upon me and the fullness of joy were wonderfully unbearable. My automatic, immediate response was deep sorrow for my weak flesh and my sinful, disobedient heart. Then, instantaneously and simultaneously, overwhelming gratitude, honor, praise, worship, and thanksgiving for His undeserved acceptance and unconditional, boundless love, flowed back to Him from the depths of my heart.

It was evident that God and the glory of His holiness were not limited or confined to the impure imperfections of earthly space, matter, or time; nor could they be limited or contained to mere humanness. The heavens were open, and God was upon us. I longed for Him to remain. I did not want to let go. I was not certain why He had chose to come, but in that awesome space of time, I was robed in His perfect love.

Though it seemed like moments, the Presence of His glory consumed us for more than six hours. It was six hours of transformation, where I was overshadowed, covered, and consumed in a pure love and divine pleasure of this all-knowing, all-holy, perfect One who formed and made me. He is the only One who knows me, all of me—my past, present, and future—and He is who I really need. In that brief open Heaven, I became intensely aware of who God really is and who I really am. My true existence was illumined. In an instant, I was gloriously "ruined" for Him. I pleaded, "To seek You, Lord, to know You is my highest aim. I lay down everything. Every part of me is Yours, Lord. If my marriage never changes...as long as I have You...please do not remove Your Presence and Your Holy Spirit from me. As long as I have You, I can want for nothing else."

In that short space of eternity touching time, the true condition of my deceived heart was bared. It became undoubtedly clear: No human relationship, no worldly possession, no human desire of any kind could or should satisfy the deepest longing of my heart and meet the greatest need of my soul. To Jesus alone belonged that honor of complete, untouched, undistracted intimacy.

The return on our feeble efforts to just respond to His initiative of love is without bounds. The Lord loves without conditions, and in His perfect purity, He loves His very life back into us. Awestruck by this amazing love of Jesus, the deathly tombstone over my heart shattered. He called me forth, exchanging my grave clothes and dressing me with His glory. Up until then, my prayers for a changed marriage had been self-directed idolatry. I wanted God to change my marriage so that I could be a "happy wife" and so that I could have a "happy family." I had been seeking the "happily ever after" blessing that I thought every Christian deserved. With deep sorrow, I confessed and repented from that sin of idolatry, which initiated the process of personal inner healing. For the first time, I could see my husband, Ché, as God saw Ché, and I wanted to love him as God loved him unconditionally.

Then and there, I wholeheartedly vowed to Jesus every part of me. Any loss, even the hope for a good marriage, was nothing compared to the gain of knowing Him. I had now tasted the depths of His love, and I knew that all other paled. Gaining Jesus means lacking nothing. Just Jesus—Jesus is enough. He is completeness. The Lord showed me there was a higher, more sacred romance, a consecrated communion with Jesus, that was incomparable with any earthly relationship. It is the relationship of the mystery of Jesus, our Bridegroom, with His glorious Bride, the Church.

Relationship is preeminent in the heart of God. God values people supremely. He proved it in His death and resurrection. The glory of God is the actual nearness and personal closeness of the unseen God. Intimate relationship is the earnest desire of God, who seeks to make Himself directly known, face-to-face, to each one of us every moment of the day and in every aspect of our lives. The Bible says that God "was made flesh, and dwelt among us," and if we "draw [near] to God...He will draw [near] to [us]" (Jn. 1:14 KJV; Jas. 4:8 KJV). He paid the ultimate price to give us this privilege of

His Presence. He sacrificed His only Son, Jesus, on the cross. He paid the highest price of love in His desire for relationship with us that the void of life would be filled with the life of God. How incredible is our God.

Our Maker created man and woman in His divine image and likeness so that we could respond to Him and fellowship with Him, and then uniquely reflect and communicate His love, glory, and holiness back to Him and to those with whom we interact. This is how we truly bring glory to His name—by being filled with Him, the essence of His glory, and sharing this knowledge of God with others. This quest for glory became my personal quest for God, my quest to know Him. I could now better identify with the apostle Paul as he said:

> But whatever was to my profit I now consider loss for the sake of Christ. What is more, I consider everything a loss compared to the surpassing greatness of knowing Christ Jesus my Lord, for whose sake I have lost all things. I consider them rubbish, that I may gain Christ and be found in Him, not having a righteousness of my own that comes from the law, but that which is through faith in Christ—the righteousness that comes from God and is by faith. I want to know Christ and the power of His resurrection and the fellowship of sharing in His sufferings, becoming like Him in His death, and so, somehow, to attain to the resurrection from the dead. Not that I have already obtained all this, or have already been made perfect, but I press on to take hold of that for which Christ Jesus took hold of me (Philippians 3:7-12).

More than ever, I need God. In my personal quest for glory, I have found Him through humility and continual repentance. For Him to increase, I must choose to decrease (see Jn. 3:30 KJV). I am continually learning that in the lowliness of humility, the grace of God abounds so that the yearning for more of Him only becomes stronger. Knowing God springs up an inner desperation to know

Him more. In desperate repentance, intercession, and fasting, we are left uncovered before the One who loves us with an everlasting love. We are as little children at the mercy and trust of our precious Father. Vulnerably bared, He then covers our fear and shame and hides us in the full protection of His unquestionable and trustworthy love. This is the holy, magnificent mystery and the highest privilege we have in union with Christ.

The brilliant beauty of this mystery is that through deep, mutual forgiveness, repentance, and reconciliation, God resurrected, restored, and renewed my husband, Ché, and myself to God and one another. We were changed in His Presence. His redemptive love caused all things to become new. Christ the Lord is the firm foundation of our marriage. A new and genuine respect and trust began to grow agape love between us where the glory of God could thrive. A true security was established in each of our hearts by the Father's love, enabling us to love each other more and give to one another freely. This same blessing is available to anyone who will call on God to do the same through the finished work of His Son on Calvary.

Ché and I continually consecrate our lives to God with the desire to become more holy and more loving. Our marriage belongs to God; it is a place where His glory is invited to inhabit. Ché and I daily choose the gift of forgiveness. We are ever learning humility through discovering our mutual need for one another and in choosing to daily receive each other. Together, we are seeking to know Him. In unity, we pray. We are being continually reconciled, man to woman, husband to wife. God offers these same privileges to all of us that each might be called a child of God. He is looking for vessels to receive His glory, vessels who want His love, vessels through which He can pour out His love upon the broken lives around us.

The Lord Jesus longs to begin with each of us, one life at a time, so that He will ultimately fill the whole earth with the glory of His Father. This is *His* quest for glory. And it begins with you and me.

Arise, shine, for your light has come, and the glory of the
Lord rises upon you. See, darkness covers the earth and

thick darkness is over the peoples, but the Lord rises upon you and His glory appears over you. Nations will come to your light, and kings to the brightness of your dawn (Isaiah 60:1-3).

America needs God like never before. Our nation has chosen to live without God, but she can begin to find Him now, one yielded heart at a time. Each of us can be a part of the solution by our own personal response to God's glory and love. Like the marriage union reveals the mystery of Christ and the Church, so, too, our individual choice to respond to God's glory and love will affect the nation and the world. God is proclaiming a wake-up call to us individually, then corporately to the Bride of Christ, then to America, and the globe. He is looking for the same humility, vulnerability, and response on every level. It is our only hope to see His glory fully come. We must humble ourselves and pray.

Experiencing His glory begins with an honest evaluation of where we are as individuals, as the Church, and as a nation. Just as I was brought to the end of myself when God urgently called to me through the weak foundation of my marriage, so to must the Church of America heed the urgent call from God now. It must begin with the *truth* that things are *not* okay in America.

It is time for us as a people to evaluate our true spiritual condition. We must seriously consider the foundation upon which this country was built. We must revisit our biblical roots, and return to Jesus Christ, our first love. We must establish God as preeminent in our nation. The starting place must be repentance in the Church of America. As God in His love has revealed self-idolatry of religion, the Bride of Christ must first repent of the idolatry of religion if we earnestly desire the glory of God to come to this nation. We, as the Bride, must become desperate for God and willing to be spent for His glory as an antidote for lost times.

But mark this: There will be terrible times in the last days. People will be lovers of themselves, lovers of money, boastful, proud, abusive, disobedient to their parents, ungrateful, unholy, without love, unforgiving, slanderous, without self-control, brutal, not lovers of the good, treacherous, rash, conceited, lovers of pleasure rather than lovers of God (2 Timothy 3:1-4).

This is the description of planet Earth today. Sadly, this is also the condition of the Church in America and in many parts of the earth. Her love has grown cold; in many regards, she is as I was—a dutiful wife with a blinded heart.

God's love can move us to change. Deeper repentance and increased prayer are our strongest spiritual weapons and greatest hope for the mercy and grace of God to bring change. We stand in a critical hour of history where the rightful judgment of God hangs in the balance all over the earth. The Holy Scriptures warn that judgment begins first in the house of the Lord, His precious Church, His beloved Bride.

The Lord is wooing us as His Bride to live out the fulfillment of Joel 2:

"Even now," declares the Lord, "return to Me with all your heart, with fasting and weeping and mourning." Rend your heart and not your garments. Return to the Lord your God, for He is gracious and compassionate, slow to anger and abounding in love, and He relents from sending calamity (Joel 2:12-13).

The choice is yours, and the time is now. May we continually give Him our hearts that He might give us His glory! May we humble ourselves daily that He might kiss the earth from Heaven in our lives, our homes, and our nation and change planet Earth! May we pray, repent, and seek Him so that we may be healed and nations may be changed...

If My people, who are called by My name, will humble themselves and pray and seek My face and turn from their wicked ways, then will I hear from heaven and will forgive their sin and will heal their land. Now My eyes will be open and My ears attentive to the prayers offered in this place (2 Chronicles 7:14-15).

We can delight His heart and answer His quest that the whole earth might be filled with His glory! It begins with you right now! May He ever find us on our knees ever desperate and grateful in our quest for glory!

A dynamic teacher of the Word, Bonnie Chavda brings revelation and release to thousands through her exciting and often dramatic exposition through her intense love of Jesus and His truth. Growing up on a ranch in New Mexico, Bonnie developed a fearless and forthright pioneer spirit. At the age of ten, a dramatic encounter with the Holy Spirit radically transformed her, causing her to totally commit her life to Christ and His purposes. A harvest of souls who will usher in the return of the Lord is now her driving passion. Bonnie has served with her international evangelist husband, Mahesh Chavda, in global mission work since 1980. The Chavdas maintain ministry bases in Central Africa and Charlotte, North Carolina, where Bonnie is the associate pastor of All Nations Church. They conduct evangelistic crusades and training seminars around the world.

Bonnie maintains a home with four children, serves as Executive Director of Mahesh Chavda Ministries International, and operates entrepreneurial enterprises. She has a deep desire to communicate the breadth, height, and depth of the love of God for His people. Her presentations as a speaker for their ministry's training conferences focus on personal revival and visitation from the Lord. Her dynamic and inspirational tapes are best sellers and are blessing thousands.

Chapter 7

Don't Miss the Glory!

Bonnie Chavda

e used to sing an old song written by Helen Howarth Lemmel that says, "Turn your eyes upon Jesus. Look full in His wonderful face. And the things of earth will grow strangely dim in the light of His glory and grace."[1] The glory of God changes the things of this earth. Moses met with God on the mountain and said to Him, "Show me Your glory" (see Ex. 33:18). The glory of God is not just a theory. It is not a word concept. The glory of God is the tangible manifest wonder of His Presence to a degree that transcends earth's bounds and makes all things possible in God.

In the glory there is joy unspeakable. In the glory there is peace unsurpassed. In the glory there are healing miracles. In the glory Heaven opens and lifts us there for a moment. In that moment the dew of Heaven waters our mortal frame and refreshes us to live in

---

1. Robert K. Brown and Mark R. Norton, editors, *The One Year Book of Hymns* (Wheaton, Illinois: Tyndale House Publishers, Inc., 1995), March 15.

God and for God in our day. Once you taste and see the glory you are forever spoiled for earth. In His Presence, hunger and thirst for more of Heaven consumes or displaces everything else. In the glory, mortals come as close to complete ecstasy and total fulfillment as is possible before we see Jesus face-to-face.

The first mention of the glory of God in Scripture comes as God wrestled to capture the heart of Israel. He had brought them out of bondage and was about to send them into Canaan to possess their inheritance. They needed to experience the glory to be changed and equipped for the journey. When the glory appeared, Israel was at an important crossroads. God yearned for them to serve Him and live. But He gave them the option to serve their own desires and reap the consequences. God wanted Israel to know the satisfaction of feeding on the glory over satisfying the gnawing hunger in their stomachs. It was this glory that God manifested in Israel's critical time. In the glory were the miracles and mantle they needed. Many who never learned this died in the wilderness.

> *...At evening you shall know that the Lord has brought you out of the land of Egypt. And in the morning you shall see the glory of the Lord....Now it came to pass, as Aaron spoke to the whole congregation of the children of Israel, that they looked toward the wilderness, and behold, the glory of the Lord appeared in the cloud* (Exodus 16:6-7,10 NKJ).

God's response to Israel's need was to manifest His glory.

Israel's testing and Israel's blessing were both in the glory! In the appearing of His glory was God's provision of miracles. But it was also a test. God sent two answers. One answer was a miraculous supply of earthly provision, namely quail, to satisfy Israel's hunger. The second was not of this earth; it was manna, God's own food from Heaven. Of these two blessings, only the heavenly one remained a blessing. Both came in the glory. However, not long afterward, the quail ceased. This was a test to prove Israel's heart and prepare them to be a people who trusted entirely upon God, a people among whom His glory could dwell continually. Israel would face greater enemies than hunger and thirst as they went forward to conquer Canaan. This was their basic boot camp. They could believe God and be sustained by the heavenly King. Or they could respond to their earthly circumstance and be subject to the kings of the earth. God could supply quail. God could send manna. When He left out quail and sent only manna, Israel rebelled. It may have been that some pestilence had infected the quail population at that time, and so to eat it would have made God's people sick. He could have sent newly created quail from Heaven. But He didn't. He gathered quail from the earth for them.

When the quail no longer came up each evening, Israel grew tired of eating only God's bread. Unbelief gave way to murmuring! They "yielded to intense craving" and complained, crying for meat as before! Meat as in Egypt! Their memory of food in bondage became sweeter than their expectation of God's provision in the land of their inheritance. In His frustration, God gave the murmurers their request. He gathered the region's quail population and dumped it on the camp of Israel. Plague followed. Those who chose quail over waiting for God died before they could chew the meat they had cried out for. How this is like society today! We seek life from the things of the earth, and the things we crave become the death of us.

For Israel, revelation, testing, provision, and the Voice of the Lord, were all in the glory. For each person, their future was decided by how they responded to the glory of God. Death or life was in the glory. Israel had quickly changed their great joyous praise for deliverance from Egypt into unbelief, murmuring, and complaining. They professed that it would be better to die in bondage with full bellies than to starve while they waited for God's provision in the wilderness. He had delivered them. Could He not feed them? They quickly became unbelieving. How earthy, how temporary, how like ourselves! Referring to this testing of Israel, Jesus prayed, "Give us this day our daily bread" (Mt. 6:11 KJV). Jesus showed us to wait for the perfect provision of God and be content. Jesus could have provided for Himself a menu to His own liking. But He asked instead for

God's choice. He taught us to live in a perpetual state of leaning fully on God in humility. He prayed, "Not my will, but Yours, God, be done" (see Lk. 22:42). Our choice is in the glory.

Our societies and the Church are standing today at the same crossroads as Israel did then in the wilderness. The needs and desires of humanity are crying out for satisfaction. If we look toward the wilderness, away from Egypt, away from all the world has to offer, away from the desires of the earth, away from the desires of the body—if we look toward faith and the eternal inheritance that God has prepared for every person in Christ, we will be filled. Our "food" is in the glory. Our life is in the glory. Our future and the future of our children are in the glory.

Have you come to an empty place in your life? Have you reached a dissatisfied season in your walk with God? Look toward the wilderness—away from all that the world can offer—to satisfy your desires and fill your needs. Look to the place where only God can be your source and supply. This is a test. You will see the glory of the Lord appear. God's answer and provision are in His glory. Respond to His glory and live. Allow Christ alone to become your satisfying daily bread from Heaven. Are you frustrated and concerned over the state of our nations and our people? Point them to the glory! Lead them to the glory. In it they too can find fullness for their emptiness, satisfaction from Heaven for the hunger in their hearts on earth.

The Hebrew word is *chabod*—GLORY! It indicates "weightiness," which refers to both presence and power. Another word for the glory of God is *Shekinah*. It indicates the manifest outshining of the virtue emanating from some source. God's glory is the influence of His manifest Presence. The outshining of the virtues of His Being pervade the atmosphere when He draws near. It was the residue of this outshining that shone on the face of Moses when he came down from Sinai. Moses' face shone like lightning. Being in the presence of God's manifested glory leaves the residue of His Presence on us. The fullness of that glory made it impossible for the priests to enter the temple at Solomon's dedication. The space was already full of something. What was it? It was the *glory!* The weight of God's glory falling made it impossible and unseemly for the people to stand in the face of the glory when it came. They fell under its weight. They bowed before its outshining.

In the history of Israel, the glory accompanied the Ark of the Covenant. The Ark did not manufacture the glory. The glory was God's manifest affirmation of all the Ark represented to the people of Israel. The Ark contained the manna that God fed Israel with. The Ark held the budded rod of Aaron's priesthood. With the manna and the rod were the tablets of the law given to Moses. The glory confirmed the covenant that the Ark indicated. The glory led Israel through the wilderness. The glory followed the anointing of the priesthood. The glory rested on and confirmed the written Word of God. In the appearance of the glory all Israel's enemies would flee. In the appearance of the glory all Israel worshiped God. In the glory God provided for His people. Jesus is the Ark of God's covenant today. Jesus is the anointed High Priest forever. Jesus is the Word of God embodied and living. Jesus is our Manna from Heaven. Where He is present, we should expect the glory of God to appear.

The glory of God is returning. Just as God sent His glory to fill the temple, He is manifesting His glory in the Church in order that the whole earth may witness it. It is the love of God in pure and personal form. When Moses chose suffering with the people of God over the opportunity of Egypt, he saw the glory of God. He exchanged the glorious earthly mantle of his inheritance as the son of Pharaoh's daughter for a simple shepherd's cloak to lead God's flock to their inheritance in Canaan. In his example, we are reminded of the apostle's words:

> *For all things are for your sakes, that grace, having spread through the many, may cause thanksgiving to abound to the glory of God. Therefore we do not lose heart. Even though our outward man is perishing, yet the inward man is being renewed day by day. For our light affliction, which is but for a moment, is working for us a far more exceeding and eternal weight of glory* (2 Corinthians 4:15-17 NKJ).

In the realm of the spirit, the glory has weight. The glory has light. It has a fragrance and a temperature. The glory has a sound. The glory has an atmosphere that is wet with Heaven's dew. We can be bathed in that dew and changed as we see the glory. It requires utter humility and childlike faith. And for many it is a test.

My first taste of the glory was in a common place—the tiny hot laundry room of our home in Ft. Lauderdale, Florida. I was sitting among heaps of dirty clothes that needed to be washed and clean clothes that needed to be folded. The rest of my family were in bed. Between the heaps of laundry sat a tiny television viewer, a notepad, and a pencil. I had been given the assignment of logging yards and yards of videotape recorded during one of my husband's evangelistic campaigns in the heart of Africa. In those days, my husband, Mahesh, would sometimes travel 250 days out of the year. I remained at home tending to our family, home, church, and ministry. Mahesh would return from the field exhausted, but with a Presence around him, a cloak of something that was not of this earth. I came to understand that Presence was the residue of the glory. Like Moses when he came down from the glory of God on the mountain, Mahesh was soaked in the glory as he was ministering the gospel to the poor and sick.

As Mahesh would come home, this Presence would, for a season, fill the atmosphere around us with a kind of supernatural light. Joy, hope, faith, and confidence from Heaven were tangible. I could have fussed and complained that I didn't ever get to go on those campaigns! I could have resented Mahesh for leaving me by myself at home with all the mundane and dirty work while he was in the glory out on the field. I could have murmured that I already had too much to do and rejected the blessing that God was bringing me in the assignment of sitting up nights logging tapes between loads of laundry! I could have been just like Israel when they rejected the manna God sent. They despised the glory and cried instead for meat. But this was a test for me. Those tapes were a medium through which God first chose to reveal His glory. In those days I knew well the promise of Psalm 68:

The Lord gave the word; Great was the company of those who proclaimed it: "Kings of armies flee, they flee, and she who remains at home divides the spoil. Though you lie down among the sheepfolds, you will be like the wings of a dove covered with silver, and her feathers with yellow gold" (Psalm 68:11-13 NKJ).

I remember the opening footage on one tape in particular. The lighting, the camera, etc., were not broadcast quality. But the images were there, living proofs of God bending down to touch desperate lives. A tall man in green military fatigues came out of the darkness carrying what appeared to be a corpse. The sick man was old and skeletal. He seemed so weak. His head fell back as the young soldier laid the old body in the dust before the ministry platform. The scene tore at my heart. Others were carried forward and laid beside the old man. The camera viewer moved on. Hours later, I was still making log entries such as: "M. preaching, little girl asleep in mother's arms, man takes notes with Bible on lap," etc. Suddenly these scenes changed. There was movement. Apparently the preaching had ended and people had begun to move forward for ministry. The air around me in that tiny laundry room began to intensify, as if still reflecting the atmosphere of the campaign on the night of the recorded images. As Mahesh came off the platform to lay hands on the masses, ushers scurried to line the people up and attempt crowd control. People began falling over. Many convulsed in deliverance. Whole groups spoke in tongues. People began to step into the light on the platform and give excited testimony of being miraculously touched in various infirm parts of their bodies. I was riveted to that tiny viewer. I could hear myself exclaiming praises to God under my breath for what I was seeing. I was sharing in the joyous spoils of Christ's victory at Calvary coming through earth's bonds and changing these lives.

All at once the camera jostled, as though the cameraman was running. The images blurred together and made me dizzy as I tried to decipher them, but only for a moment. Then, out of the blackness came the old man whom I had seen carried in at the beginning of the tape. Standing upright on his own, the white-haired man grinned brightly from ear to ear. He held his arms in the air and joyously marched into the light in triumph! Others around him rose from their mats as God also touched them. The man in military fatigues came running into the picture. He marveled jubilantly at the old man. The old man walked back and forth as if testing the new life in his limbs and body. Then the young man testified. The old man was his father. The son had gone from his military post to the hospital and carried his dying father to the crusade. All earthly hope for the old man had been gone. The family had expected the father to die within hours from the disease that had invaded his frail body. The old man lay, like Aaron's rod, lifeless in the Presence of the Lord. The gospel was proclaimed. Then the glory touched him. That lifeless, fevered body was healed! I wept and rejoiced as I watched father and son embrace in the fuzzy images on that tiny video viewer. I responded to the glory!

That response secured for me a future when I would see and experience the glory of God firsthand on the mission field. It came in the next few years as Mahesh made plans to return to Africa. The ministry was in need for funds to hire a camera crew. But Mahesh was determined to bring back video testimony of the great things God would do. It occurred to Mahesh that I would be an economical "crew" to take along. I did not require separate lodging. I had the constitution to do with little and give 110 percent without complaint or rebellion. I learned how to operate a camera and I flew with him to Zaire! Remembering the work of recording those first videotapes, I determined to make a written daily record of what we saw and experienced. My journal reads:

> "I am writing by candlelight. The hotel's only power source, a generator, is not working. They have not needed it till now for some time anyway. Our plane trip via single-engine plane into the interior was very loud, bumpy, crowded, and hot. Mahesh, Maki, M'Poy, and I held various pieces of equipment for the crusade as weight allowed. As we circled the airstrip beyond Kikwit, a thick bank of brightly dressed citizens waving palm fronds and long bouquets of flowers greeted us, looking up at our tiny aircraft. Their bodies gyrated in rhythm, and I knew that they were singing. 'No video anywhere on the airfield!' our pleasant

Canadian pilot shouted over the roar of the plane's engine. 'This is a military installation. Very tight. Very paranoid about security.' [How often I was thus instructed in various stops in this country.] Our arrival was celebrated by dozens of tiny, dusty children scantily covered in rags, and slightly older children in worn school uniforms. Classes were turned out to greet us. It seemed the whole city came out to line the dirt road from the airfield to town. Women, young and old, dressed in bright African costume carried flowers for us. Young men in simulated western dress that appeared to be pieced together from used polyester passed down from the sixties ran alongside as our motorcade wound into town. They sang in Lingala and shouted, 'Allelujah! The servant of God has come!' It was very humbling.

"Day 2: Our hotel water supply is rainwater stored on the roof and released each morning, unfiltered and unheated. With a huge rattle of the otherwise empty pipes the water rushes into the commode. A housemaid appears to turn on the taps in the bathtub and fill it for our use throughout the day. This is our only water. All bathing, shaving, laundry, etc. for both Mahesh and myself is done with this tubful. We quickly devise the schedule of who bathes what first, right down to laundry, all of which is done after our personal needs are finished. Every room has an air conditioner, but the hotel is without the power to run them. It is stifling. If we open the windows, our room quickly fills with voracious mosquitoes. Maki is working on finding parts to repair the hotel power supply. Dinner by candlelight! Our meal is daily plain boiled spaghetti, a boiled chicken (I think) that is quite impossible to cut, and tea made from grass. Occasional rats scurry along the baseboard. At just before 3:00 a.m. I awoke to intense burning, itching misery covering my body. My flashlight revealed angry red welts from head to toe. I looked like I had chicken pox—and itched the same! In my angst I accidentally awakened Mahesh who returned to the battle for the skin of his face and head against the mosquito Luftwafa diving above him. Throwing back the bedclothes, I discovered brown spots of dried blood from some past hotel guest. I fumbled to find the Cutter's repellent and smeared on another layer. I imagined bed bugs. Then I discovered an outpost of ants beneath my bed. Covering my bed with my raincoat and using my formerly slept-in shirt for a pillowcase, I tried to return to sleep.

"4:30 a.m. Mahesh was awake and scratching. After my revelations he said, 'I don't want to know why I am scratching.' Those dried blood spots haunted us. It was pitch black still. African night sounds filled the air. A rooster crowed in the neighboring compound. 'Your dinner tonight,' Mahesh mumbled, '...is calling to you!' I laughed.

"6/22: Crusade—logistical difficulties bring us to the crusade later than our intended start time. We have only two hours of daylight left. Every moment lost robs us from ministering to the many desperately sick people after the preaching. Mahesh insists on laying hands on each of them individually. I ventured into the thick crowd, but it caused such a commotion that I felt it best to retreat to the platform area and gather video footage from there. Mahesh preached a very powerful and concise message on Jesus as the only Savior and the necessity for every person to make a choice to accept and follow Him or to reject and suffer the consequences, presently and for eternity. Thousands responded. Decision cards were dispersed, and our army of ushers and counselors moved through the mass of raised hands. Mahesh led in a prayer of repentance and salvation and then welcomed the Holy Spirit. The Lord began to walk among the people. Waves of tongues rolled forth from the crowd. Then the miracles came. A woman with rheumatism was healed. A 30-year old man with AIDS testified of experiencing a complete change in his body. Words of knowledge from Mahesh spoke to barrenness and various diseases. The bugs swarmed out of the night toward our camera lights. They flew up our noses, into our ears, and crawled through our hair while we tried to get steady shots of these miracles! The atmosphere all around us was electric! There was an excited swell of bodies towards the back of the crowd. We looked toward the commotion and watched the crowd part in jubilation. People were jumping and shouting. They moved aside to reveal a small boy rigidly and solemnly marching toward the platform. His eyes were fixed on us. As he came into the open, the crowd went wild. They knew this child. The faces of the sponsoring pastors went wide in awe. This boy had been crippled from birth. Crippled that is, until the glory touched him tonight! Behind the camera lens, my tears blurred the frame.

"6/23: Crusade—it was astounding. As the video confirms, there were numerous major miracles. Two children, a little boy brought by his friend and a nine-year-old girl brought by her sister, both deaf and dumb from birth, demonstrated they could now hear and speak! The little girl was terrified of the video light but clearly repeated the words spoken to her. The little boy began making vocal sounds although he was not speaking clearly. His friend said to Pastor M'Poy, 'This is my friend. He has been unable to hear or speak since he was born. I thought, *I am sure that Jesus will have mercy on him.* So I went to his house and brought him here.' The boy who brought his formerly deaf friend had a bandaged foot. On Tuesday we will water baptize the new Christians.

"6/25: Departure: An entourage of local pastors and officials found transportation to the airfield to bid us farewell. Mahesh sat with Kibala (our main local sponsoring pastor) for a few minutes to thank him and give further instructions concerning the new converts. We told Kibala that we would begin to send him monthly financial help. He was visibly moved. He became very silent and tearful as he accepted this good news. I have learned that Kibala works tirelessly seven days a week with his own church and five others he has planted in this city. In addition to that, he travels often, walking to oversee and nurture churches in 14 villages in the Bandundu Province. Many who attended our crusade and Bible foundation seminars here walked two to four days through the jungle to come. They slept in the open field, found bread from local vendors, and filled themselves on the Word of God and glory manifested throughout the campaign. They tell us they are 'going home full!'"

I saw the glory firsthand. In those moments, every year of labor for the Lord at home in my long wait to come to the field was suddenly worth it, and a small price to pay for those glorious moments. I tasted the true bread that comes down from Heaven. I was satisfied. No complaining for me! I was in the glory, and there is nothing else like it on earth!

I experienced the glory in my own body in a different way during the ordeal of the birth of our fourth child, Aaron, in 1985. I turned up pregnant as we were planning Mahesh's second trip to Africa. Usually that's good news. But in this case, I started bleeding heavily in my second month. Tests concluded that I had a severe case of placenta previa centralis. In other words, the placenta, which nourishes and develops the child en utero, was lying on the bottom of my womb over the opening. My every movement strained the placenta and robbed our baby of full en utero support. I was ordered to complete bed rest and soon began experiencing premature labor. My obstetrician discussed with us the risks and dangers of my situation to my life and health. Beyond that, he gave us no reasonable hope the pregnancy would last more than a few more weeks. He stated, "If it does continue, by some miracle, there are high possibilities the child may have severe birth defects or serious disabilities." He sadly recommended a DNC.

We responded, "We will wait for awhile and see what the Lord does." I went to bed, and Mahesh became Mr. Mom. Everything went downhill from there. If things were bad, they got worse. If circumstances were against us already, they moved to formidable and beyond—to completely impossible. God said nothing. It was a test. I cried out to God day and night. My strength was failing. Hemorrhaging, contractions, pain, and feebleness increased in my body. Mahesh prayed and prayed for the Lord to intervene. It seemed like time passed by in slow motion. By now the doctors said that the baby was surely dead and we should go ahead with the operation to clean and restore my womb.

Then the Lord gave us the wisest secret battle weapon—hilarity. It was during those dark days that the Lord told Mahesh, "Laugh!" He led us to break the heavy ominous atmosphere of the physical truth, the doctor's prognosis for me, and the helpless tiny life in my womb by listening daily to Bill Cosby tapes! As Bill described his trips to the dentist, raising his children, and feeding his children chocolate cake, and smearing Jell-O on the floor to ward off the giant chicken heart, Mahesh and I would shake with laughter. We went through each day clinging to the Lord and His daily manna to sustain us.

One day, as I was laying in bed praying for our outreach to Africa (I had determined that the more the devil attacked, the more I would intervene in prayer for the helpless and poor who were waiting in Zaire for the Lord's touch), the Lord spoke to me. It was that still, small voice that often sounds just like me but has a sense in it that lets you know that it's really Him. He told me: "You will have a son. Name him Aaron. For I will take him and make him a sign. And I will make his rod to bud as I did with Aaron of old."

I was impressed to read Numbers 17 where I saw the miracle of Aaron's priesthood in the Presence of the glory of the Lord. I was sure that people would think I was a senseless fanatic if I told anyone what I had heard. But I desperately wanted to believe it was really God who had come and given me this promise. The very next day, an old friend whom I had not seen for years called me from

Texas. She said she was praying for me and had received "a really weird word." It was the kind of thing, she said, that she would never presume to say to anyone. I could hear the trepidation in her voice and knew she trusted our friendship enough to proceed: "I heard this: that you are going to have a son. And you should name him Aaron."

Not long after that, something terrible happened. On one trip to the bathroom, which by now was my only time out of bed, something slipped out of my body and into the water of the commode. Terror gripped me. Darkness surrounded me. I fully expected to turn to see my dead child! I wept. I felt so alone and so afraid. I was forced to kneel down and retrieve whatever it was that had fallen out of my womb. It was a large unidentifiable mass. But it was not my baby! As it turned out, the placenta was working so hard at trying to save this child that it was disintegrating. A part of it had broken off and fallen out. Not more than a few days after this my contractions that had continued off and on became very intense. It seemed that everything was out of time. I was rushed to the hospital. My doctor's main fear was that, because of all the heavy bleeding already experienced, emergency surgery and a transfusion might not be enough to save my life in this crisis. In addition, against all conventional wisdom, Mahesh was out of the country preaching a crusade in the Antille—at my encouragement!

The night before my appointed surgery, I had a dream. I was flying in the Presence of God over a grand, vast, snow-covered mountain wilderness. Mountain goats skipped on the rocky slopes below me. Suddenly there was a sound—unlike any earthly sound; it was the sound of power coming out of the depths of the Lord's Being. It was His Voice. This wave of energy caused the side of a mountain to break away and fall into the treescape below. It was not devastating; it was magnificent. God was playing! In the dream, I heard the words from Psalm 29:3-4,8-9 (NKJ):

The voice of the Lord is over the waters; the God of glory thunders....The voice of the Lord is powerful....The voice of the Lord shakes the wilderness....The voice of the Lord makes the deer give birth...and in His temple everyone says "Glory!"

The next day was the fortieth anniversary of the day on which the Allied Armies crushed the grip of Nazi Germany and rolled in to liberate Europe. The television was filled with scenes of the days when concentration camps were opened, and emaciated, weeping prisoners came forth to life and freedom. It was a day when God finally rescued His people, the Jews, from a hand that had been too strong for them. As I watched, I knew that the birthday of my son, whom God had said would be a sign, was intended for that day. I was rolled into the operating room and surrounded by emergency teams who were to attempt to help in the delivery of my son. But Someone besides the medical teams and myself entered at the same moment. As the anesthesiologist prepared his sleeping potion for me, that "Fourth Man" in the operating room came near me. I felt the wave of the sound that I had heard in my dream come through my body like waves of light. The "Fourth Man" was speaking. As He was with Daniel in the lion's den, as He was with Daniel's friends in the fiery furnace, He was with my unborn son and me. When those light waves passed through my body, my mouth opened, and I heard myself say to my obstetrician and to the anesthesiologist who were prepared to do an emergency c-section, "I can have this baby naturally." Everyone stopped and looked at me. A calm filled the room. They looked at one another and back at me. "Okay," my doctor replied.

The next thing I remember was hearing five tiny mews, like those of a newborn kitten. They were the sound of my son's voice! My doctor's visage turned ashen as the baby appeared. It was obvious that in the natural, things looked very grim. The neo-natal unit rushed in. But I looked at the shaken face of the doctor and said, "It's a boy, isn't it?" He nodded yes. "His name is Aaron," I said. On the day Aaron was born, I was four months short of a nine-month term.

I died once during that lengthy trauma. My spirit left my body in the midst of intense pain. As I was ascending, I became acutely aware of the burden Mahesh would have to embrace if I did not stay behind and help him with our family and ministry. I saw my children crying for their mommy. I returned! The glory of God had overwhelmed all earthly authority and circumstance, including doctors' plans and convention, and my own feeble body, in order to accomplish the desire of God.

Little Aaron weighed less than a pound. All strikes were against him by the time he had been on earth for three weeks. But he was alive! It took nearly six months of intensive care for Aaron to reach the five-pound mark and be released to go home. One Sunday morning, when Aaron was not yet released from the hospital neo-natal care unit, the Lord said, "Aaron will be a sign, a sign of My glory in My Church at the end of the age—a Church who outwardly appears to be born before the fullness of time, feeble and diseased, in danger of blindness, gangrene invading its inward parts, body systems broken down, and unable even to breathe on its own strength. (These were just some of Aaron's difficulties.) It will be as Aaron's rod that, in a single night, budded and bore fruit as it lay in the Presence of My glory. And that tiny Church shall arise, a light in the midst of deep darkness, even as when the Allied Armies fought the formidable foe of Nazi Germany and counter-invaded Europe to set My people free—free from death camps, free from the domination of evil. My Church shall arise and shine to set the captives free! As you watch Aaron grow, be assured that I will do this thing in My Church!"

As of this writing, Aaron is 14 years old. He is an "A" student, a brilliant thinker and artist, gentle and humorous. He is gifted in music and is excelling in self-defense training. He has a servant spirit. He is obedient to his parents, working without complaining and obeying without question. In recent days, Aaron has begun to bud in true prophetic insight and sensitivity to the Holy Spirit. Aaron is a sign of the Church that is rising! He has recently entered a growth spurt, and with that, impressive muscular development is occurring! Maybe you feel you are like Aaron when he was born: All odds are against you. You are like someone born before his/her time. But God has ordained your life. You will arise and shine. Step into His glory! Let His glory put life into your death. Let His glory heal your disease. Let His glory put strength in your weakness. Let His glory make the rod of your life bud as He did with Aaron. Let His glory carry you to inherit your promises and fulfill your destiny in Christ!

Jesus prayed, "Your will be done on earth as it is in heaven" (see Mt. 6:10 NKJ)! God's will was not for Aaron to die. God's will was not for me to die. God's will was not for Aaron to be blind or left physically and mentally devastated by the death and disease that assailed him. God's will was to manifest His glory in both Aaron and me! God's will was to make us, by those very sufferings, a testimony to His glory! God's perfect will was accomplished in the glory! The sufferings we experienced weighed down on us at times, as though we had no hope. The pain in our physical beings sometimes seemed to defy life itself. The devil assailed and persecuted our minds and emotions with his threats of death and the impossibility of our circumstance. Had God deserted us? No! He was setting us up to experience His glory! It was only a test. Are you suffering today? Are you being persecuted by the enemy and oppressed in your mind? Has all the earth can offer failed you? Look toward the wilderness and witness His glory. Choose life. Eat the bread that will come to you from Heaven and be satisfied. As the Bible says, "Do not cast away your confidence, which has great reward. For you have need of endurance, so that after you have done the will of God, you may receive the promise" (Heb. 10:35-36 NKJ).

The Church, for the most part, has been a place manifesting only a form of godliness with no power (see 2 Tim. 3:5). The Church, much less the world looking on, has seen little of the glory of God. But God has declared that a day would come when His people will arise and shine with the glory of the Lord. Those days are upon us. Isaiah says that the appearing of this glory will be in the midst of a time of intense darkness over the peoples of the earth, a time like today. (See Isaiah 60:1-2 NKJ.) Then God's redeemed ones will arise in His glory. The Scriptures indicate the restoration of God's anointed priesthood. This priesthood will declare and prepare the way for the High Priest of their faith, Christ, who is coming to sit as King forever over the nations of the earth.

The *chabod* of God has long been absent from the Church. God's glory had also departed in the day of the priest Eli. But God's glory is returning again, no less than it did in Solomon's day. In fact, Scripture prophesies that the return of God's latter glory will be greater than the glory of Solomon's temple! God is rebuilding and refurbishing His dwelling place—His redeemed people! Just as He has said, "The glory of this latter temple shall be greater than the former" (Hag. 2:9 NKJ). A greater One than Solomon is here— Jesus, our High Priest, who reigns and offers prayers on our behalf before God perpetually! Now, a new Church is emerging on the earth, a Church of believing saints whose lives are being touched by the glory. It is a Church that is changed, renewed, commissioned, anointed, and released to do exploits in the glory. (See Daniel 11:32 NKJ.)

For these reasons, as well as many more proofs, I believe that God's answer for our sin and need today is not judgment first. I believe that God's first act will be to show us His glory. He will show Himself in His great love and let the people, everyone and everywhere, make the choice for themselves. Then will come the judgment—life to those who choose wisely and the wages of sin to those who reject His glory when He comes. In this season, God's answer for society's yielding to intense craving and sin is not destruction:

> *For God so loved the world that He gave His only begotten Son, that whoever believes in Him should not perish but have everlasting life* (John 3:16 NKJ).

> *But God demonstrates His own love toward us, in that while we were still sinners, Christ died for us* (Romans 5:8 NKJ).

> *But now the righteousness of God apart from the law is revealed....even the righteousness of God, through faith in Jesus Christ, to all and on all who believe. For there is no difference; for all have sinned and fall short of the glory of God* (Romans 3:21-23 NKJ).

Just like Israel in the wilderness, society has failed to look to the glory of God for its solutions and satisfaction. But as we come to the crisis of sin that seeks to overwhelm our nations and our lives, God once again is sending His glory!

At the end of the ministry of the priest Eli, the ark of God was captured by Israel's enemies and the *chabod*—the glory—departed from Israel. Eli's daughter-in-law, Phinehas' wife, was with child and due to be delivered. When she heard the news that the ark of God had been captured and that her father-in-law and husband were dead, her labor came upon her. She delivered a child. As the woman was dying she named the child *I-chabod*, "the glory has departed"! (See First Samuel 4:19-22.) Before Eli died, God told him: "I will raise up for Myself a faithful priest who shall do according to what is in My heart and in My mind. I will build him a sure house, and he shall walk before My anointed forever" (1 Sam. 2:35 NKJ). These words prophesied of Samuel, of Solomon and his temple, and ultimately of Christ, the anointed Son, God's High Priest, and our King, and of His Church.

Eli's charge, young Samuel, arose to restore the anointing to the priesthood. Samuel anointed Saul to be king and David after Saul. David restored the ark to Jerusalem. But it was when the temple was finished and dedicated that the glory returned to dwell among the people of God. Upon completion of all these events, Solomon prayed and dedicated the dwelling place to the Lord. God reconsecrated the priesthood with fire from Heaven and confirmed it with His glory. The glory of God filled the temple. The appearance of His glory caused thanksgiving, praise, and worship in the hearts of the people who witnessed the return of the glory.

> *When Solomon had finished praying, fire came down from heaven and consumed the burnt offering and the sacrifices; and the glory [chabod] of the Lord filled the temple. And the priests could not enter the house of the Lord, because the glory of the Lord had filled the Lord's house. When all the children of Israel saw how the fire came down, and the glory of the Lord on the temple, they bowed their faces to the ground on the pavement, and worshiped and praised the Lord, saying: "For He is good, for His mercy endures forever"* (2 Chronicles 7:1-3 NKJ).

As great as this restored Presence was, God has said, "The glory of the latter house," the Church yet to arise, "will be greater than the glory of the former" of Solomon's temple! (See Haggai 2:6-9 NKJ.) How will God do it? "The silver and gold belong to Me," the Lord told His prophet (see Hag. 2:8). The means by which this reconstruction and rededication of God's dwelling place attains greater glory will be entirely the Lord's doing!

In 1994, our family and ministry moved to Charlotte, North Carolina. In those first few weeks, the glory of the Lord began to spontaneously show up in various rooms of our new house. Together with workers and friends, whenever this happened we would stop whatever we were doing and wait in the glory! In the glory the joy of the Lord, the spirit of prophecy and revelation, and the spirit of prayer, would descend upon us corporately. Sometimes those moments turned into six-hour Holy Ghost banquets! We converted the horse barn on our new property into a small, primitive church. There, we began keeping the Watch of the Lord—an all-night prayer and worship gathering each Friday night. Now, in the midst of eight hours of concentrated corporate praise, worship, thanksgiving, supplication, intercession, and prophetic proclamation of the word, we find ourselves in the glory! If you come and listen, if you come and watch, if you come and enter in, you will see the glory of God. At times, you will experience no less than that Presence of His Glory that came on us in Africa or that saved me and my infant son in that hospital in Florida. In recent months, the dramatic miracles of healing and deliverance are increasing—miracles in America! We've witnessed healing from cancer, diabetes, asthma, and more. As the glory has continued to fall around us, a most unusual thing has come in the glory—gold flecks of metallic dust that rise out of the pores of the worshipers in the Presence of the Lord, and with that, gold fillings in people's teeth. With man these things may seem suspicious, fruitless, and flamboyant, but God loves them. And when five-year-old Maggie's asthma leaves forever in that same Presence, when 19-year-old Daniel rises out of a coma in that same Presence, and when an 80-year-old grandmother is completely healed of stomach cancer in that same Presence, we know that we are in the glory of the Lord. These miracles accompany His glory. The mercy of God is being manifest in His glory. We used to see these things in the Third World only. Now the glory is coming to America, too! God is manifesting His glory according to His own delight, and with it He is delighting the hearts of the simple who are eagerly waiting, like hungry children, for His glorious appearing!

This is the generation of John the Baptist before the great and terrible day of the Lord. If we listen we will hear:

The voice of one crying in the wilderness: "Prepare the way of the Lord; make straight in the desert a highway for our God. Every valley shall be exalted and every mountain and hill brought low; the crooked places shall be made straight and the rough places smooth; the glory of the Lord shall be revealed, and all flesh shall see it together; for the mouth of the Lord has spoken" (Isaiah 40:3-5 NKJ).

God's answer to the cries of this generation, which are rising to the Heavens, is to send His glory!—just as He did when Israel cried for bread and meat in the wilderness. King David knew the glory of God. David knew that his victory was in the glory. He knew that even in times of utter failure and desperation, his deliverance and provision would be found in the manifest glory of God. Consider the last of David's recorded songs, where he writes,

Give the king Your judgments, O God, and Your righteousness to the king's Son. He will judge Your people with righteousness, and Your poor with justice.... For He will deliver the needy when he cries, the poor also, and him who has no helper. He will spare the poor and needy, and will save the souls of the needy. He will redeem their life from oppression and violence; and precious shall be their blood in His sight....And blessed be His glorious name forever! And let the whole earth be filled with His glory (Psalm 72:1-2,12-14,19 NKJ).

How fitting these words are for our generation. As David completes his discourse, in the very last line of all of his prayers, he says, "Let the whole earth be filled with His glory!" The glory is coming to your heart. The glory is coming to your house. The glory is coming to your church. The glory is coming to your town. Don't miss the glory! When we find Him, we find true riches. When He comes near, He shows us His glory. And indeed, the words of the song ring true, "The things of earth will grow strangely dim, in the light of His glory and grace!"

Other *Destiny Image* *titles* you will enjoy reading

THE DELIGHT OF BEING HIS DAUGHTER
by Dotty Schmitt.
Discover the delight and joy that only being a daughter of God can bring! Dotty Schmitt's humorous and honest anecdotes of her own life and struggles in finding intimacy with God will encourage you in your own personal walk. Now in the pastoral and teaching ministry with her husband Charles at Immanuel's Church in the Washington, D.C. area, Dotty continues to experience and express the joy of following her Father.
ISBN 0-7684-2023-7

HINDS' FEET ON HIGH PLACES (Women's Devotional)
by Hannah Hurnard.
What can be more exciting than the *Hinds' Feet on High Places* allegory? It is the allegory along with a daily devotional for women by a woman who has proven her walk with the Lord and her writing gift with other inspirational books. Most of these devotions are "quiet time" meditations, ones that will draw you closer to your Lord Jesus. They will help you to understand your own struggles and regain confidence in your walk with the Lord. This allegory with the devotionals will help satisfy the yearning of your heart. He is challenging you to keep saying "yes" to your Lord as He beckons you on in your own journey to the High Places.
ISBN 0-7684-2035-0

WOMEN ON THE FRONT LINES
by Michal Ann Goll.
History is filled with ordinary women who have changed the course of their generation. Here Michal Ann Goll, co-founder of Ministry to the Nations with her husband, Jim, shares how her own life was transformed and highlights nine women whose lives will impact yours! Every generation faces the same choices and issues; learn how you, too, can heed the call to courage and impact a generation.
ISBN 0-7684-2020-2

THE ASCENDED LIFE
by Bernita J. Conway.
A believer does not need to wait until Heaven to experience an intimate relationship with the Lord. When you are born again, your life becomes His, and He pours His life into yours. Here Bernita Conway explains from personal study and experience the truth of "abiding in the Vine," the Lord Jesus Christ. When you grasp this understanding and begin to walk in it, it will change your whole life and relationship with your heavenly Father!
ISBN 1-56043-337-X

Available at your local Christian bookstore.

Internet: http://www.reapernet.com

Other *Destiny Image titles* you will enjoy reading

THE GOD CHASERS (Best-selling **Destiny Image** book)
by Tommy Tenney.
There are those so hungry, so desperate for His Presence, that they become consumed with finding Him. Their longing for Him moves them to do what they would otherwise never do: Chase God. But what does it really mean to chase God? Can He be "caught"? Is there an end to the thirsting of man's soul for Him? Meet Tommy Tenney—God chaser. Join him in his search for God. Follow him as he ignores the maze of religious tradition and finds himself, not chasing God, but to his utter amazement, caught by the One he had chased.
ISBN 0-7684-2016-4

GOD CHASERS DAILY MEDITATION & PERSONAL JOURNAL
by Tommy Tenney.
ISBN 0-7684-2040-7

GOD'S FAVORITE HOUSE
by Tommy Tenney.
The burning desire of your heart can be fulfilled. God is looking for people just like you. He is a Lover in search of a people who will love Him in return. He is far more interested in you than He is interested in a building. He would hush all of Heaven's hosts to listen to your voice raised in heartfelt love songs to Him. This book will show you how to build a house of worship within, fulfilling your heart's desire and His!
ISBN 0-7684-2043-1

Available at your local Christian bookstore.

Internet: http://www.reapernet.com

Other
Destiny Image titles
you will enjoy reading

THE POWER OF BROKENNESS
by Don Nori.
Accepting Brokenness is a must for becoming a true vessel of the Lord, and is a stepping-stone to revival in our hearts, our homes, and our churches. Brokenness alone brings us to the wonderful revelation of how deep and great our Lord's mercy really is. Join this companion who leads us through the darkest of nights. Discover the *Power of Brokenness*.
ISBN 1-56043-178-4

ENCOUNTERING THE PRESENCE
by Colin Urquhart.
What is it about Jesus that, when we encounter Him, we are changed? When we encounter the Presence, we encounter the Truth, because Jesus is the Truth. Here Colin Urquhart, best-selling author and pastor in Sussex, England, explains how the Truth changes facts. Do you desire to become more like Jesus? The Truth will set you free!
ISBN 0-7684-2018-0

POWER, HOLINESS, AND EVANGELISM
Contributing Authors: *Gordon Fee, Steve Beard, Dr. Michael Brown, Pablo Bottari, Pablo Deiros, Chris Heuertz, Scott McDermott, Carlos Mraida, Mark Nysewander, Stephen Seamands, Harvey Brown Jr.*
Compiled by *Randy Clark. Randy is also the author of "God Can Use Little Ole Me."*
Many churches today stress holiness but lack power, while others display great power but are deficient in personal holiness and Christian character. If we really want to win our world for Christ, we must bring both holiness and power back into our lives. A church on fire will draw countless thousands to her light.

"Caution: The fire in this book may leap off the pages on to the reader. God's fire empowers, purifies, and emboldens our witness. This is the way the Church is supposed to be. Highly recommended."

—Dr. Bill Bright, Founder and President
Campus Crusade for Christ International

"The future of the Church is at stake and this book has some answers."

—Tommy Tenney, Author of *The God Chasers*

ISBN 1-56043-345-0

Available at your local Christian bookstore.

Internet: http://www.reapernet.com

Other
Destiny Image titles
you will enjoy reading

THE LOST PASSIONS OF JESUS
by Donald L. Milam, Jr.
What motivated Jesus to pursue the cross? What inner strength kept His feet on the path laid before Him? Time and tradition have muted the Church's knowledge of the passions that burned in Jesus' heart, but if we want to—if we dare to—we can seek those same passions. Learn from a close look at Jesus' own life and words and from the writings of other dedicated followers the passions that enflamed the Son of God and changed the world forever!
ISBN 0-7684-2045-8

A DIVINE CONFRONTATION
by Graham Cooke.
The Church is in a season of profound change. The process is sometimes so bewildering and painful that we don't know which way is up or down! Here's a book that separates truth from feelings and explains the elements involved in transition. Its prophetic revelation and deep insight will challenge your "church" mind-sets and give your heart much food for thought. This book is a must-read for all who want to know what is happening in the Church today!
ISBN 0-7684-2039-3

FATHER, FORGIVE US!
by Jim W. Goll.
What is holding back a worldwide "great awakening"? What hinders the Church all over the world from rising up and bringing in the greatest harvest ever known? The answer is simple: sin! God is calling Christians today to take up the mantle of identificational intercession and repent for the sins of the preset and past; for the sins of our fathers; for the sins of the nations. Will you heed the call? This book shows you how!
ISBN 0-7684-2025-3

THE MARTYRS' TORCH
by Bruce Porter.
In every age of history, darkness has threatened to extinguish the light. But also in every age of history, heroes and heroines of the faith rose up to hold high the torch of their testimony—witnesses to the truth of the gospel of Jesus Christ. On a fateful spring day at Columbine High, others lifted up their torches and joined the crimson path of the martyrs' way. We cannot forget their sacrifice. A call is sounding forth from Heaven: "Who will take up the martyrs' torch which fell from these faithful hands?" Will you?
ISBN 0-7684-2046-6

Available at your local Christian bookstore.

Internet: http://www.reapernet.com

Other
Destiny Image titles
you will enjoy reading

AN INVITATION TO FRIENDSHIP: From the Father's Heart Volume 2
by Charles Slagle.
Our God is a Father whose heart longs for His children to sit and talk with Him in fellowship and oneness. This second volume of intimate letters from the Father to you, His child, reveals His passion, dreams, and love for you. As you read them, you will find yourself drawn ever closer within the circle of His embrace. The touch of His presence will change your life forever!
ISBN 0-7684-2013-X

HIDDEN TREASURES OF THE HEART
by Donald Downing.
What is hidden in your heart? Your heart is the key to life—both natural and spiritual. If you aren't careful with your heart, you run the risk of becoming vulnerable to the attacks of the enemy. This book explains the changes you need to make to ensure that your commitment to God is from the heart and encourages you to make those changes. Don't miss out on the greatest blessing of all—a clean heart!
ISBN 1-56043-315-9

DREAMS IN THE SPIRIT, VOL. 1
by Bart Druckenmiller.
We all want to hear the word of the Lord. Nevertheless, many people don't. They limit how God speaks, not recognizing His voice throughout life's experiences, including dreams in the night and "daydreams" born of the Spirit. As a result, our lives lack vision and destiny. This book will introduce you to how God speaks through dreams and visions. It will give you hope that you, too, can learn to hear God's voice in your dreams and fulfill all that He speaks to you.
ISBN 1-56043-346-9

DREAMS IN THE SPIRIT, VOL. 2
by Bart Druckenmiller.
Broaden your scope and let your dreams soar—shrug off that narrow thinking! God's view of your life on earth is much bigger than your small earthly view of Heaven. Your dreams give you a peephole into God's large perspective, and they can expand your possibilities in the spiritual realm! Experience a fresh view of life from a much higher plane in *Dreams in the Spirit, Volume Two.*
ISBN 1-56043-347-7

Available at your local Christian bookstore.

Internet: http://www.reapernet.com